PASTORAL FOUNDATIONS OF THE SACRAMENTS

A Catholic Perspective

Gregory L. Klein, O. Carm.
and
Robert A. Wolfe, O. Carm.

PAULIST PRESS

New York/Mahwah, N.J.

The Publisher gratefully acknowledges use of the following: Scripture excerpts are taken from the *New American Bible with Revised New Testament* Copyright © 1987, 1970 Confraternity of Christian Doctrine, Washington, D.C. Used with permission. All rights reserved. No part of the *New American Bible* may be reproduced or transmitted by any means without permission in writing from the copyright owner. Excerpts from the English translation of the *Catechism of the Catholic Church* for use in the United States of America © 1994, United States Catholic Conference, Inc.–Libreria Editrice Vaticana. Used with permission. Excerpts from the English translation of *Rite of Marriage* © 1973, International Committee on English in the Liturgy, Inc. (ICEL); excerpts from the English translation of *Rite of Confirmation*, Second Edition © 1975, ICEL; excerpts from the English translation of *Ordination of Deacons, Priests, and Bishops* © 1975, ICEL; excerpts from the English translation of *Pastoral Care of the Sick: Rites of Anointing and Viaticum* © 1982, ICEL excerpts from the English translation of *Rite of Christian Initiation of Adults* © 1985, ICEL. All rights reserved. Excerpts from *Vatican Council II: The Conciliar and Post Conciliar Documents,* New Revised Edition, edited by Austin Flannery, O.P., copyright © 1987, Costello Publishing Company, Inc., Northport, N.Y. are used by permission of the publisher, all rights reserved. No part of these excerpts may be reproduced, stored in a retrieval system, or transmitted in any form or by any means–electronic, mechanical photocopying, recording or otherwise, without express permission of Costello Publishing Company. Excerpts from *Doors to the Sacred: A Historical Introduction to Sacraments in the Catholic Church* by Joseph Martos © 1991 and published by Triumph Books are used with permission. Excerpt from *Ministry: A Theological, Pastoral Handbook* by Richard P. McBrien © 1987 and published by HarperCollins Publishers is used with permission.

Cover design by James F. Brisson

Library of Congress Cataloging-in-Publication Data

Klein, Gregory L., 1947–
    Pastoral foundations of the Sacraments : a Catholic perspective / Gregory L. Klein and Robert A. Wolfe.
        p.   cm.
    Includes bibliographical references.
    ISBN 0-8091-3770-4 (alk. paper)
    1. Sacraments–Catholic Church. 2. Catholic Church–Doctrines. I. Wolfe, Robert A., 1947– . II. Title.
BX2200.K55   1998
264'.0208–dc21   97-41747
                                                                              CIP

Published by Paulist Press
997 Macarthur Boulevard
Mahwah, New Jersey 07430

Printed and bound in the
United States of America

Contents

Dedicated to
Lawrence and Eileen Klein
and
F. Kenneth and Virginia Wolfe

Introduction

In his novel, *The Forgotten,* Elie Wiesel tells the story of an aging father struggling to remember the cruelties he endured during the Holocaust and share them with his son. It is a story filled with faith and hope, guilt and despair; a story focused on the truths which bind one generation to another. The situation of the story in the intimacy of family, the obscurity of politics and the mystery of religion enables the reader to explore the vital importance of remembrance in human experience. Wiesel begins the novel with a passionate prayer to God:

> ...God of justice, be just to me. God of charity, be kind to me. God of mercy, plunge me not into...the chasm where all life, hope and light are extinguished by oblivion. God of truth, remember that without memory truth becomes only the mask of truth. Remember that only memory leads man back to the source of his longing for You.
>
> Remember, God of history, that You created man to remember. You put me into the world, You spared me in time of danger and death, that I might testify. What sort of witness would I be without my memory?
>
> Know, God, that I do not wish to forget You. I do not wish to forget anything. Not the living and not the dead. Not the voices and not the silences. I do not wish to forget the moments of abundance that enriched my life, nor the hours of anguish that drove me to despair.
>
> Even if you forget me, O Lord, I refuse to forget You.[1]

In significant ways remembrance is the heart of Catholic worship. While worship arises out of our contemporary experience, it connects us to a past which is treasured for its impact on our present and its hope for our future. Worship enables us to remember a God who holds us in the palm of his hands, a God who molds and shapes us as a potter shapes the clay, at first fragile and ugly but eventually strong and noble, a God who never forgets so that we can always remember. Catholics celebrate the joy of birth in baptism to remember that God is the author of all life. Catholics celebrate the sadness of death in the Order of Christian Funerals to remember that God promises a life that is changed, not ended. Catholics celebrate the incredible love of a man and a woman in marriage to remember that God's love for us is beyond what we can imagine. Catholics celebrate their unity in the eucharist to remember that God is the source of all that binds us together. In the human experience of life and worship Catholics give witness to the truth that only memory can treasure.

In this book we propose a model for exploring and understanding Catholic worship. Catholic worship focuses on the celebration of the sacraments, the principal acts of worship in the Catholic community. The model begins with the human experience of persons who come to the church for a variety of reasons and occasions. Many chapters will begin with an actual pastoral situation, though the names have been changed, adapted from the experience of the authors. The model then proceeds to an examination of the sacraments as we find them rooted in the ministry of Jesus, the foundational experience of the church, and then to a brief review of the history of the sacraments in the church. Finally, the model focuses on the actual rites of the church and some of the pastoral challenges Catholics encounter in their efforts to live the truth that only memory can treasure. Throughout this book we make reference to the wealth of doctrinal and catechetical material contained in the *Catechism of the Catholic Church,* the church's latest reference text, to continue to enable the renewal of the whole life of the church.[2] All of the chapters in this book end with "Questions for Reflection and Discussion." Our hope is that readers will find these questions helpful for integrating the material into their own experiences of worship and for discussing with others the many challenges and implications for Christian life which worship presents us.

Pastoral Foundations of the Sacraments is an attempt to connect human experience, theology and pastoral practice. We will investigate Catholic worship and the sacraments from the perspective of human experience, with attention to the pastoral implications of current sacramental and liturgical theology. Academic theology is a vital and necessary part of our study, but it is equally necessary to examine the actual liturgical rites and contemporary human experience to enable us to grasp the depth and breadth of Catholic worship.

Chapters one and two will explore worship and ritual from the history of religion's point of view. The goal of these two chapters is to explore human experience as the starting point for an examination of the "holy." This leads quite naturally to an examination of such topics as "sacred time," "sacred place," "sacred objects," and "sacred persons." Here we consider such foundational concepts as the kingdom of God, the call to conversion, the nature of worship, including the Jewish roots of Christian worship, and a working definition of sacraments. These chapters set the stage for an exploration of the primary sacramental rites of the church.

Chapters three through ten will explore the sacraments as the typical and ordinary ways Catholics worship. Each of these chapters will consider: (1) the origins of the sacrament in Jewish worship and the ministry of Jesus; (2) the major historical developments of the sacrament; (3) the theology of the actual rituals and prayers of the sacrament as currently celebrated; (4) the pastoral challenges in the celebration of the sacrament in the Catholic community today. This exploration of the sacraments will require locating each sacramental rite in the ordinary human experience of people who constitute the community of faith. Chapter eleven, "The Ritual Life of the Parish," addresses the old and the new ways ordinary Catholics express their faith. In the final chapter we draw together some of the principal insights of our study which we believe can enhance the ordinary life of worship within the Catholic community.

We believe that several primary groups of people will benefit from our study of Catholic worship. One group is students in introductory level courses in worship and sacraments. Few college students major in theology or religious studies. Most students in Catholic colleges and universities are required to take a few introductory level courses in religion or theology. The scope of these courses tends to be rather broad and general. Yet these students will most typically encounter the church through their experiences of worship—Sunday eucharist, weddings, funerals, baptisms, confirmations, etc. They have a need to understand worship and the sacraments as rooted in their own human experience and linked to a community of faith which has its roots in Judaism and the experience of Jesus Christ.

Another group who can benefit from this volume is adults engaged in parish life. Many adults serve their local parish community in a variety of ways as lectors, extraordinary ministers of the eucharist, ministers to the sick and dying, religious education teachers, etc., and have little practical knowledge of worship or formal theological training. They have a need to understand the human experience of worship and the rich history and tradition of worship within the Catholic community.

We write from within our own Roman Catholic perspective because we believe *Pastoral Foundations of the Sacraments* will benefit Catholics in understanding their own religious tradition and its impact on their own human experience. Catholic sacraments are part of a larger Christian and religious tradition which we share with millions of people in the world. We believe that in understanding a part of that tradition we can come to understand something of what we share with many people in the world.

1

The Human Experience of Worship

*J*ennifer was six years old. Her family was on vacation in Colorado. They had been enjoying the fresh air, the mountains, and the streams. Jennifer's father had told her that the thing to do in Colorado was to pan for gold. He had purchased some "fool's gold" from the local souvenir shop. Every morning he would place some in the bubbling brook behind their condominium. Jennifer would take her pan down to the stream and would pick up the silt and swash it around over and over again, moving up and down the stream until she would inevitably find the gold. With a great sense of accomplishment she would run to her parents and shout, "I have found another one!" They were amazed at her excitement each day as she searched for her treasure in the refreshing waters.

The other family members were taken by the vistas of Colorado. They stared at the mountain peaks and marveled at the wonders of the pine forest. Jennifer, however, remained fascinated by those things that were at her feet. While Dad pointed out soaring eagles, Jennifer had her eye out to see if there was more gold in the stream.

Jennifer got up early one morning and was very anxious to head down to the stream for her daily search. She found her father at the dining room table with road maps spread out before him. He also had a ruler and seemed to be measuring something. He gave Jennifer a big good morning kiss and said to her, "Jennifer, I'm going to show you the Grand Canyon. I just figured it out. We can drive there in just a couple of days!" Jennifer could not understand why her father was so anxious to leave this wonderful place where you could find gold in really cold water. Much to the surprise of the whole family, the father loaded everyone into the car that morning and they headed off to Arizona. He kept telling them that visiting the Grand Canyon had been his life-long dream. They would have a lot to tell their friends when they got back home to New Jersey.

Jennifer cried as they pulled away from their vacation home. She said she was worried that others would come and take her gold. Her father told her that it was just "fool's gold" and that he had been putting it in the stream to amuse her. He said that it was time for her to stop looking at the ground and to start seeing the wonders of the land in Colorado and Arizona.

Jennifer had a very hard time understanding adults. She sat in the back of the car and mumbled and groaned and fought with her sister. She could not appreciate her father's enthusiasm for this trip. The car was hot. She kept looking out the window and mistrusting the world where stones that look like gold are not gold at all.

Along the way they stopped at Monument Valley. Her father and mother kept pointing out the mountains that appeared to be thrusting themselves out of the desert floor. They kept calling to Jennifer to look this way or that. Jennifer kept looking at the ground. She was fascinated by an Indian who was nearby selling jewelry from the back of a truck. She found a melted tip of a Bic pen on the ground. She ran to her father and said, "Look, Daddy, I found turquoise!" Her father made her get back into the car.

The trip was much longer than the father had expected. They arrived at the rim of the canyon way after dark. Since they had not made plans for a hotel, they had to sleep in the car overnight. Jennifer was tired of getting yelled at. She made the best of a bad situation. She cuddled in her mother's arms and asked with as much exasperation as a six-year-old could muster, "Why is Daddy making us do this?"

It was still dark when the father got the family up. He was in a big hurry. "We have to go to the edge of the canyon right now," he said. Jennifer wondered why her father wanted her to look up at things, because sleeping in a car and getting up when it is still night sure didn't make any sense.

When they arrived at the edge of the Grand Canyon they met many people doing the same thing. Families were gathering. Children were crying. There was a great sense of anticipation in the air. Very gradually the night sky began to lighten in the east. First it was pale blue, then there was some gold. Finally the sun rose above the horizon and began to splash wonderful color on the black abyss before them. Moment by moment the canyon began to appear before their eyes as if being painted by a magical brush. The crowd became very quiet. Jennifer climbed up into her father's lap and with a great deal of breath said, "Daddy, look! It's so beautiful!" Her father drew her in close. Their two faces began to shine as they too were painted by the sun.

When the sun was fully up and the Grand Canyon in full view before them, all of the people began to applaud and cheer the wonderful show they had seen. Jennifer took her father's hand as they got up. "Daddy," she said while squeezing his fingers, "this was really holy. I think it's really good to look up." Her father placed a comforting hand on her shoulder and said: "Yes, honey, this was really holy."

The Nature of Human Experience

Our ordinary human experience teaches us something about worship because we have all had experiences of worshipping. *Webster's Dictionary* defines worship as reverence for a deity or sacred object; a set of religious forms by which this reverence is expressed; intense devotion to or esteem for a person or thing; attendance at a religious service. The object of worship can be God, another person, or some object. One of the aims of celebrating eucharist is to worship God; one of the aims of marriage is for a man and a woman to reverence one another through a life of love and devotion; one of the aims of many people is to treasure certain material objects—the picture of a deceased loved one, a family heirloom passed down through generations, or a precious work of art. While the object of worship is ideally something worthy of respect and reverence, we know from our experience that some people worship objects which, in the realm of things important, do not seem all that worthy of respect and reverence. Some people worship themselves to the exclusion of others. Some people worship their homes, their cars or their money—objects which, while valuable in themselves, are transitory and fleeting. A culture caught up in materialism can easily place a value on things as opposed to persons, on one culture as opposed to other cultures, on one class of people as opposed to other classes of people. The object of worship is not always something all people believe is worthy of respect and reverence.

Our human experience teaches us that one of life's tasks is the discernment and discovery of that which is really valuable and important for us. All experience is initially a trial, test or proof. Human persons are, in one sense, "bundles of experiences." Growing through life stores up experiences which we continually fall back on to move forward in trial, test or proof. Some of life's experiences prove helpful, others unhelpful. We judge some of our experiences positive, others negative, and still others neutral. We generally reverence and respect those experiences which prove to be positive, those experiences which move us in the direction of healthy growth and development, in the direction of understanding, compassion and empathy. Reflection on our life's experiences helps us to interpret our experiences, select critical values, and move into the future as persons of integrity. For Christians, Jesus of Nazareth is an object of worship because he reflected on his life's experiences, selected the values critical to his understanding of his vocation as a child of God, and moved into the future, even a future which included death, because of his personal integrity and devotion to God.

It is possible to discover the object of our worship, that which we reverence and respect, by simply reflecting on our life's experiences. It is impossible to reflect on all of our experience because in one sense we are bombarded with experience all of the time. But all of us naturally reflect on those experiences which have a profound effect on us or those experiences which shock us because of their extraordinary nature. A very common example of this is the death of a loved one. The death of a loved one is usually a shock to us and an occasion for us to begin to reflect on our relationship with the loved one. We begin to remember our experiences with the loved one and tell the stories of our friendship and love. Reflection on these past experiences leads us to articulate the values which motivated our friendship and love. As our reflection reveals the values which we treasured in the relationship with the loved one, we begin to compare these values with the culture in which we live and with our religious values and convictions. We may begin to see the deceased loved one as a real encounter with God. We begin to understand the love and forgiveness of God because of the love and forgiveness shared in friendship. We begin to understand the challenge of living the values of the gospel because of the challenge of living faithfully in friendship. This natural process of reflection on significant life experiences leads us to reverence and respect a set of values which we look for in our relationships with other people. It leads us to understand and reverence our religious values and enhances our understanding of the gospel. Conversely, this reflection enables us to reject cultural and religious values which are not consistent with our experience.

The Revelatory Nature of Human Experience

One of the distinguishing characteristics of Christians is that, through their critical reflection on life experience, they acknowledge God as the origin of all that exists and the object of their worship. As Christians reflect on their life experiences, they tend, more often than not, to recognize the presence of God, gently yet powerfully guiding the moments and movements of their lives. Christians recognize that Jesus Christ is the fullest revelation of God; and so, the imitation of Christ, under the guidance of God's Spirit, becomes their lifelong task. Christians value the Bible as the "word of God" and understand the revelation of God both in the Old Testament, the story of God's revelation to the Jews, and the New Testament, the story of God's revelation through Jesus and those who initially followed him. The imitation of Christ has very practical implications for Christians. They read and reflect on the Bible and look for the values which seem to characterize those people who were faithful to God. Old Testament stories which articulate the justice and care of God for all of God's people lead Christians to select the values of justice and care for all people as goals worthy of imitation and implementation in their daily lives. New Testament stories that show Jesus urging his followers to forgive enemies and to take care of strangers challenge Christians to choose the way of forgiveness and devote time and money to improving the plight of poor persons—goals which they deem worthy of imitation and implementation in their daily lives. Through reflection on their life experience, Christians tend to reject cultural values which do not reflect these religious values. Excessive materialism, warlike aggression between and among nations, and government which benefits the rich and ignores the poor are some examples of cultural values which Christians find contrary to the teaching of the Bible. For Christians, God and the values of God are the only true object of worship, reverence and respect.

Another distinguishing characteristic of Christians and many other religious people in the world is the belief that God can be known through ordinary human experience. The pastoral situation at the beginning of this chapter is an example of this. During the course of a family vacation, Jennifer's father gradually and gently leads her from the experience of a sunrise over the Grand Canyon to an experience of the holy. Christians use the word *sacrament* to designate those human experiences which Christian tradition testifies are almost sure to reveal the presence of God. Paul Tillich, a Protestant theologian, provides the following definition of sacraments:

> Any object or event is sacramental in which the transcendent is perceived to be present. Sacramental objects are holy objects, laden with divine power.[1]

Many religions have sacraments in Paul Tillich's sense of this term, but only Catholics use the word sacrament.

The word *sacrament* comes from the Latin word *sacramentum*. Both before and after the life of Jesus, Israel was occupied by the Romans because Israel was part of the great Roman Empire. For the Romans, *sacramentum* referred to a pledge of money or property which two parties left in a temple prior to a lawsuit or contract, and which was forfeited by the one who lost the lawsuit or broke the contract. *Sacramentum* later came to refer to the oath of allegiance which Roman soldiers made to their commander and the gods of Rome. During the second century Christians borrowed the term and used it to explain the ceremony of Christian initiation. Just as Roman soldiers pledged their allegiance to the Roman emperor and the gods of Rome, so too Christians pledged their allegiance to the God of Jesus Christ. As Christians gradually became the largest religious denomination in the Roman Empire, the Roman usage of *sacramentum* disappeared and the Christian usage dominated. By the fifth century St. Augustine used the word *sacrament* to refer to any sacred symbol or ceremony which was a sign of sacred reality. It was not until the twelfth century that the word *sacrament* was more restricted and applied to the seven church sacraments we have come to know: baptism, confirmation, eucharist, reconciliation, anointing of the sick and viaticum, marriage and holy orders.[2]

The word *sacrament* is now restricted to religious designations. *Webster's Dictionary* defines sacrament as a formal Christian rite, such as baptism or marriage, especially one thought to have been instituted by Jesus Christ. Sacraments are signs or symbols of sacred reality. Every religion in the world has times, places, objects and persons that are signs and symbols of sacred reality which point beyond human experience.

Rites of Passage and Rites of Celebration

Our human experiences teach us that there are special times in our lives, times distinguished from the ordinary and the routine, which focus our attention on the sacred, holy and mysterious. Anthropologists and sociologists have traditionally identified these special times as "rites of passage" and "rites of celebration." Every culture and society celebrates the special times which mark the various passages in life from birth to death.

Rites of passage are public ceremonies which mark a change in a person's life. Ancient cultures celebrated puberty rites to mark the passage from childhood through adolescence to adulthood. Nations celebrate the crowning of a monarch or the inauguration of a president to mark the passage from ordinary citizenship to publicly recognized leadership of a people. A man and a woman publicly celebrate a wedding ceremony to mark the passage from single life to married life. In older cultures and civilizations rites of passage were fundamentally religious ceremonies; in modern secular cultures and civilizations vestiges of these religious ceremonies and customs can be seen in baby showers, presidential inaugurations, fraternity and sorority initiations and funerals. Rites of passage are social rituals which publicly symbolize and dramatize some change in social status. The Christian sacraments function, in part, as rites of passage. The sacrament of baptism publicly symbolizes and celebrates the initiation of a person into the church. The sacrament of marriage publicly symbolizes the covenant of lifelong, unconditional love between a man and a woman. The *Order of Christian Funerals* publicly symbolizes the passage of a person from this life to life with God.

Rites of celebration are public ceremonies which celebrate some permanent reality or value, which although always present is sometimes forgotten. People naturally want to celebrate birthdays, anniversaries and national holidays, like Independence Day. Rites of celebration remember past events of great significance—the birth of a child, the wedding of a man and a woman, the revolution which brought freedom. These past events call to mind beliefs and intensify values which continue to have great meaning to those who celebrate them. The Christian sacraments function, in part, as rites of celebration. The most obvious example of this is eucharist. Christians gather to celebrate eucharist to participate in the paschal mystery of Christ in word and bread and wine, and to renew their baptismal promises to follow Christ, to preach his word and to be bread and wine for one another. In the sacrament of reconciliation Christians celebrate their lifelong commitment to accept God's gracious forgiveness of their faults and failings, and to rededicate themselves to moving away from sin and selfishness toward compassion and forgiveness in their relationships with one another.

Sacred Times, Places, Objects and Persons

Recently, Catholic theologians and educators have leaned heavily on sociological interpretations of ritual and worship. Sacramental ceremonies can be understood as symbolic expressions of sacred realities which are recognized and accepted by people of faith. And so, for example, baptism signifies a cleansing from sin and a reception into the Christian community. Eucharist symbolizes the presence of Christ and the unity of the church in the community of faith. Marriage is a sign of a real change in the relationship of two persons to each other, to God, and to society. The realities symbolized are social realities because they are recognized and accepted by the believing community. But they are also transcendent realities because their author and cause is God.

Catholic sacraments function in this way—both sociologically and theologically. Catholic sacraments are social ceremonies which manifest the religious experience of a believing people.

Both our human experience and our religious experience teach us that certain times, places, objects and persons are special and significant. There is something about human experience which draws us out of the simple and the ordinary and into the special and the significant. Sometimes, something so simple and ordinary as a family vacation becomes revelatory of the beauty and wonder of God. Some times, spaces, objects and persons can be sacred. In the history of religions this notion is captured by the word *hierophany*—a manifestation of the sacred. Experiencing sacred times, places, objects and persons is like discovering a whole new world of meaning. Catholic theologian Joseph Martos, in his book *Doors to the Sacred: A Historical Introduction to Sacraments in the Catholic Church,* begins his exploration of Catholic sacraments by reviewing the research of Mircea Eliade. Eliade has studied how sacramental rites and objects function in a variety of religions and cultures. According to Martos, sacraments function as "doors to the sacred." Sacraments are invitations to religious experience. Because sacramental celebrations arise out of human experience, they are dependent on time, place, objects and persons.[3]

We ordinarily experience time as continuous—sometimes it passes quickly, sometimes it drags—but always there is time, one moment following another. On certain occasions our consciousness of time is altered and we enter a special time, a sacred moment. Parents usually remember the time their child was born as special and sacred. Children usually remember the time their parents died; this dreaded time is special and sacred. These special and sacred moments in time feel different from many other times in our lives. When we remember these times, the past is suddenly *now.* This is the sense of time in sacramental experiences—precious time, eternal significance.

Sacred space functions in much the same way. Space is

space, and most of the time we take the spaces we inhabit for granted. We live in some spaces, work in other spaces, and vacation in still other spaces. At certain times, however, space is vitally important. Some spaces feel different from other spaces. After a long time away from home, our home feels special and significant. Catholics go to the Holy Land, Jews go to Jerusalem, and Muslims go to Mecca—all of these spaces are special and significant to those who believe in them. We visit the Grand Canyon, a towering cathedral, a national shrine, the grave of a loved one, and these spaces feel very different from the ordinary spaces we inhabit. Some spaces have the ability to put us in touch with the sacred and the special, generally because of important events associated with those spaces. Some spaces are imbued with significance and put us in touch with the sacred and the holy.

In a materialistic culture, objects often have little significance. Many of the things we have and use are disposable—they are designed to become obsolete and unusable. We discard so many objects that we now have to invent new ways to dispose of our garbage, or learn how to recycle it. But inevitably, nearly every person treasures certain objects. Some treasured objects are valuable because they are really precious—a crystal vase, a gold watch, a Picasso painting. Other treasured objects are valuable because they were given to us by a special person on a particular occasion—an engagement ring, an autographed book, a family picture passed down from one generation to the next. These objects are ordinary by comparison, but because of the meaning they hold for us, they are special and sacred. When we look at these objects, when we touch them, when we contemplate their meaning, they put us in touch with sacred reality.

During the course of a lifetime, we encounter many persons and treasure only a handful. Many of the people we encounter in the daily course of life are insignificant to us. But some persons are very significant and sacred. We treasure the persons who gave us life and nurtured us. We may even remember a teacher or a pastor who so profoundly influenced us that the courses of our lives were changed. We treat monarchs and presidents with special respect, even though we may have never met them. Nearly every religious tradition in the world pays special attention to some persons designated to symbolize the values, attitudes and beliefs of that religion. And so, priests, rabbis, ministers and shamans have a special respect and reverence attached to them. Some persons are treasured because they, more than any other person, help us encounter the special and the sacred in human life.

Human experience thrives on special times, places, objects and persons; without these life would be rather dull and boring. And so, it is no surprise that an integral, sustaining feature of religious experience is sacred times, places, objects and persons. In the Catholic imagination sacraments function to put us in touch with those special and sacred times, places, objects and persons which form the foundation of our Catholic faith. When parents bring an infant to their parish church for baptism, they are responding to God's invitation to see in this event of birth a manifestation of the presence of God in their lives, and in the life of the church. The day of baptism, celebrated in their parish church, with oil and water, by their parish priest, in the company of their family and friends and fellow Christians, is a sacred event; these factors coming together is no accident. These are deliberate decisions by people who are trying to respond in faith to the presence of God in their ordinary human experience. The gestures, actions, objects and words, spoken or written—the sounds and smells, and persons and places surrounding the baptism function to make this experience a sacramental encounter. The mystery of birth is celebrated within the context of a religious ritual which, on the one hand, makes sense to the believing community, and on the other hand, puts us in touch with the mystery of God, which we will never fully comprehend.

Summary

Quite ordinary human experience is the root and foundation of our worship, which arises quite naturally and spontaneously from the routine of our daily living. Human experience gives rise to deliberate associations of meaning with certain particular experiences. Often, these special and sacred meanings are associated with both ordinary and extraordinary moments in our lives, which give shape and purpose to our existence. The Catholic imagination puts us in touch with a tradition which has always seen special times, places, objects and persons as revelatory of God. Sacraments are "doors to the sacred"—invitations to religious experience.

Questions for Reflection and Discussion

1. Try to remember a *significant experience* from your life and recall as many details as possible. Try to capture your feelings about this experience, then and now. Why is this experience so powerful and significant for you?

2. Try to remember a *significant religious experience* from your life and recall as many details as possible. Try to capture your feelings about this experience, then and now. What made this experience so powerful and significant for you? Why do you describe this experience as "religious"?

3. Discuss some times of profound change in your life. How did these times of passage affect you? Were you fearful? Were you energized by them? Did you celebrate or ignore these times?

4. Share some of your experiences of Catholic sacraments. Have you witnessed a baptism, confirmation, or first communion recently? What is your response to this experience?

2

The Religious Experience of Worship

*B*ill hadn't been to church in over twenty years. He just got out of the habit of going. When asked, he would always say that he was a Catholic. He thought of himself as a Catholic and enjoyed telling stories about his experiences with the nuns in his school. He had been close to one of the priests in his parish. He had fond memories of his first communion and confirmation. He was married in the church by his friend, the priest. Over the years, however, he just drifted away.

Bill celebrated his forty-third birthday alone. His marriage had failed. He had lost contact with his son. He had a few friends, but didn't bother to tell anyone it was his birthday. He sat at the kitchen table sipping a beer. He allowed the silence of the summer night to comfort him.

Bill had been daydreaming for a good while. He finished his beer and stood up to stretch and suddenly a profound feeling of loneliness came over him. He sat down again and thought, "I must put my life back together again." He thought about a variety of things he could do or places to go that would reconnect him with people. He had joined some clubs over the years, but they too were ultimately uninteresting. He began to think about his youth and the comfort he used to feel going to church. The weekend was coming up. He decided to go to his old parish for mass.

On Saturday evening, Bill got out his white shirt and set out a tie he hadn't worn for years. He was surprised at how excited he was to be going to church. He wondered whether he would recognize anybody from his old neighborhood. He remembered the sound of the beautiful organ, the smell of old incense, and the beautiful statues. He was feeling very good about himself and his decision to reacquaint himself with his church. Sunday would be a very good day.

Bill called the parish on Sunday morning and was surprised to find out that his old parish had only two masses on Sunday. He was also surprised that he had gotten that information on a tape. He wondered what would happen if he had an emergency. He dismissed his random thoughts and straightened his tie and headed off for church.

He was surprised at how the neighborhood had changed. Some houses were gone. Some new businesses were in place. He parked close to the church and with a sense of purpose quickly made his way into the building. He always sat on the left side of the church near the back. He was disappointed that a large Oriental family was in his place. He moved across the aisle and sat down. He was a bit bewildered. He didn't recognize anybody. He was looking at the congregation and was amazed at the variety of people who were in church. St. Mark's was originally a German ethnic parish and Bill remembered that mostly German families attended. What he saw this Sunday morning was a mix of Oriental and Hispanic people.

He settled down and began to look around. Most of the statues were gone. There was no smell of incense. A woman came out and began to practice some music while she accompanied herself on a guitar. He was becoming very uncomfortable.

Suddenly he became aware that there was an old woman staring at him. He looked back at her and recognized that it was his old next door neighbor. She came over to him and embraced him. Bill coughed and straightened his tie. She said, "Welcome home, Bill." Bill sighed with relief and sat down.

Mrs. Keller sat with Bill and showed him how to go through the missalette. As the mass unfolded, Bill began to smile. The place was very different, yet very much the same. It wasn't the music or the statues, it was a chance to pray again and meet his God. At the sign of peace he kissed Mrs. Keller on the cheek and, with some extra breath, said, "Thanks." Mrs. Keller used the tissue she always had with her to wipe the tear from the corner of his eye.

The Kingdom of God

Sacraments are "doors to the sacred"—invitations to religious experience. For Christians, Jesus Christ is the model and pattern for responding to God's invitation to experience life from the perspective of God. The stories of the New Testament tell us that when in the presence of Jesus people experienced life, and their relationship to God, in a new way. In the presence of Jesus people felt like they belonged (baptism); they felt affirmed (confirmation); they felt a sense of fellowship, unity and bondedness (eucharist); they felt incredibly loved (marriage); they felt destined and called (orders); and they felt healed and forgiven (anointing and reconciliation). While the words the church has used to name these sacramental experiences were probably not the words Jesus himself used, it is such experiences of fellowship and love and forgiveness, etc., which are clearly rooted in the preaching and ministry of Jesus. It is in this sense that Jesus is the author of the sacramental experiences which are such an integral part of Catholic life and worship.[1]

The New Testament preserves the church's record of Jesus' response to God's invitation to experience all of life from the perspective of God. Each of the synoptic gospels (Matthew, Mark and Luke) presents the theme of Jesus' preaching and teaching—the kingdom of God. Although few Americans have ever experienced rule by a king, Catholics and other Christians find the kingdom of God a familiar term. We pray the "Our Father," a prayer centered on God's kingdom, and petition, "Thy kingdom come." Nathan Mitchell, in his book, *Eucharist as Sacrament of Initiation,* has said that in the gospels Jesus is attentive to the ways of the world and to the ways of God in that world. The central theme of Jesus' preaching and teaching, the kingdom of God, is an invitation to conversion. The parables of Jesus present the process of conversion as a call to transition, hope and courage.[2]

Methodist theologian James W. Fowler has given a handy definition of the kingdom of God in his book, *Weaving the New Creation: Stages of Faith and the Public Church.* Fowler suggests that the *kingdom of God* is the *commonwealth of justice and peace that God intends for all the world.* In other words, God intends that the wealth of all the people of the world must be justice and peace. Allegiance to the kingdom of God includes conversion to the idea that God has structured in nature and history an all-inclusive justice. God is the spirit who, in many subtle and convergent ways, inspires the maintenance and transformation of the world.

God is the power of a future commonwealth of love and justice, envisioned and enacted by Jesus, that is already breaking into and transforming nature and history.[3]

Catholic theologian Francis Schussler Fiorenza suggests that, rather than defining the kingdom of God, we focus on its characteristics. He believes that biblical scholars today indicate that scripture does not so much define the term as describe its various and multiple dimensions. Fiorenza believes that the kingdom of God is real, inclusive and demands solidarity, that it requires a transformation of the world and of all creation, and that it is of invaluable worth and has an incalculable future.

The kingdom of God is *real* in the ministry of Jesus. The gospels make this point by stressing the activity of Jesus, especially his exorcisms, healings, and table fellowship. "The blind regain their sight, the lame walk, lepers are cleansed, the deaf hear, the dead are raised, and the poor have the good news proclaimed to them" (Mt 11:5). Jesus does not merely announce that God's kingdom will come; his words and actions demonstrate with real power that the kingdom has come and is still coming.

The kingdom of God *is inclusive* and *demands solidarity.* God invites into the kingdom all the people of the world; no one is excluded. In fact, God seems most concerned with those whom most of us don't want to be concerned with—the sinners and tax collectors, the prostitutes and the marginalized. God seeks the lost, the abandoned and the excluded. Once people accept the invitation to God's kingdom, rigorous requirements follow. The members of the kingdom of God are an unlikely assortment of individuals who are called to live in solidarity with one another. Membership in the kingdom of God is based on a diversity which is marked by solidarity.

The kingdom of God is not opposed to the world and creation as we know it. However, the kingdom of God demands a *transformation of the world and of all creation.* God chose to inaugurate the kingdom here and now, in the world and creation as we know it, but its fulfillment requires a radical change in our relationship to the world and creation.

The kingdom of God is of *invaluable worth* and has *an incalculable future.* Many of the parables of Jesus describe the invaluable worth of God's kingdom—a great treasure or a great pearl (Mt 13:44, 45). And the kingdom has a future, a future that is not subject to our control. The fulfillment of God's kingdom is beyond our power to imagine it. In the future, God will bring reality, already present in Jesus, to fullness.[4]

These many dimensions of the kingdom need to be kept in tension in order that the building of God's kingdom, the commonwealth of justice, love and peace, may come about in a future yet to be realized—and probably beyond our wildest imagination.

The Call to Conversion

In worship, Christians respond to God's invitation to the kingdom through the transformation of the world and all of creation. The scriptures provide the pattern and the model for the kind of conversion required.

Christians believe that God's saving activity of election, exodus, assembly, covenant and passover is accomplished and brought to fulfillment in the ministry, passion, death and resurrection of Jesus. The parables, those stories spun from the ordinary stuff of human experience, point to these mysteries of human life. The parables speak not so much of historically true events, but rather of profoundly true human experience.

Many Christians have had the experience of reading or hearing some of the parables of Jesus, and thinking, "That doesn't make any sense." It is similar to the experience of reflecting on our own lives and thinking, "My life doesn't make any sense." The pastoral situation at the beginning of this chapter is a good example of this. Bill's life was falling apart. Celebrating his forty-third birthday alone was the occasion for a transformation of his life. Bill's conversion was rooted in his experience of loneliness and confusion. The parables of Jesus, like life itself, often leave us with questions rather than answers. Human experience is inherently narrative in form. Our lives are not played out in logical sequence but in the mystery of story. The primary purpose of the religious stories of the Bible is to transform us. We know that our lives are saved and transformed not so much by ideas but by living faith.

Jesus demonstrates the mystery dimension of election, covenant, and assembly in his parables. The parables of the lost sheep (Lk 15:1–7) and the lost son (Lk 15:11–32) draw us into the mystery of the assembly, elected by God and in covenant with God. The shepherd who leaves the ninety-nine sheep to seek and find the one lost sheep is not providing good evidence of careful shepherding, but rather demonstrating the love of a God whose willingness to risk is beyond the bounds of logic. The lost younger son and the lost older son are not good examples, respectively, of what it means to be unfaithful or faithful to a parent, but rather demonstrate the profound mystery that real faithfulness sometimes includes unfaithfulness. Being lost is generally an unpleasant yet inevitable human experience. Being found and rescued from the grip of selfishness and sin is a profound human experience few of us could survive without. God's word saves us precisely because we are lost and cannot save ourselves. Salvation comes in spite of us, when we recognize that we are lost, and when we are open to being found.

Israel's story of the exodus functions as a paradigm for our Christian journey of salvation. It is interesting that God chose the people of Israel, assembled them at Sinai, and made a covenant with them. Some of the early writers of the church believed that the desert, the wilderness, had been created as supremely valuable in the eyes of God precisely because it had no value to people. The wasteland was the land that could never be wasted by people, because it offered them nothing.

The desert was the place where the people of Israel had wandered for forty years, cared for by God alone. They could have reached the promised land in a few months had they travelled directly to it. But God's plan was that they should learn to love God in the wilderness and that they should always look back on the time in the desert as the idyllic time in their relationship with God. The desert was created simply to be itself, not to be transformed by people into something else.[5]

The Gospels tell us that Jesus spent considerable time in the desert, to be in communion with God. It was not so much that Jesus could not find God in the cities and towns, the people and events of his ordinary life, but that he needed to discover what he really hungered and yearned for. Desert solitude cures the desire for fame and fortune, for friendship and love, for success and privilege.

The man who fell victim to robbers as he went down from Jerusalem to Jericho (Lk 10:29–37) should have been able to rely on the priest and the Levite, rather than on the Samaritan to come to his assistance. One rarely believes that salvation can come from one's enemies. Sometimes our hope is misplaced. In the desert, filled with nothing and fraught with despair, we come to find that in God alone rests our hope. As we wander in the desert, and gradually become one with its silence, our hearts are finally open to listen to the word of God. God's saving word transforms us into a people who together open our minds and hearts to be elected and assembled, and to play our part in God's saving activity in the world.

The church as people of God assembles to hear and take to heart the saving word of God through corporate ethical commitments and ministry. Within this people of God, there is a diversity of functions and roles, but a unity of spirit and purpose. As Paul says there is one spirit but many different gifts. There is one Lord but many different ministries. Though there is a diversity of works it is the one God who accomplishes all of them in everyone. Central to Paul's faith and teaching is that the different gifts and ministries and works are given to each person for the common good. Paul uses the image of the human body to illustrate his point of unity in diversity. One human body with many different parts is for Paul an apt symbol of the unity in diversity which characterizes the church. The different parts work together in harmony for the proper functioning of the body. All of the parts are equal in importance. Through baptism into Christ, all of the diverse members of the church, male and female, Jew and Greek, slave and free, young and old, rich and poor, form the one church of Jesus Christ, a unity in diversity (1 Cor 12:4–7, 12–13).

The biblical notion of assembly is, therefore, a key and fundamental notion in our understanding of church. We are most fully church when we are gathered together as a people in eucharistic assembly. In many ways the Sunday eucharistic assembly is the oldest activity of the church.

The earliest followers of Jesus continued the practice of participating in the synagogue assembly on the Sabbath, and met in the eucharistic assembly on Saturday evening or Sunday morning. As the emerging church began to understand its own unique identity, the Sabbath assembly fell by the wayside, leaving the Sunday eucharistic assembly as the distinguishing feature of the Christian community. They assembled on the first day of the week because it was the day God inaugurated creation and the day Jesus rose from the dead.

The Sunday eucharistic assembly on the first day of the week was profoundly important to Christians because they lived in the world in dispersion. Christians were not distinguished from other persons by country, language, clothing or race. Both men and women, both slaves and free, both Jews and Gentiles were included in the assembly. Christians did not lose their identity while living under these conditions because of the Sunday eucharistic assembly.[6]

While Christians found within the assembly relationships of love and friendship, the overwhelming bond which united the eucharistic assembly was the bond of joy which faith gives. Those who assembled for eucharist had to do a certain violence to the social order that reigned in their everyday lives. Rich and poor, slaves and free, men and women, friends and strangers, Jews and Greeks set aside social, cultural, political and economic norms in order to unite themselves in a community of love. The eucharistic assembly makes the church visible as a community of love. In this way, it once again challenges society's inequities by becoming the place for the redistribution of goods.

The radical nature of the Sunday eucharistic assembly is dramatically portrayed in Matthew's parable of the judgment of the nations (25:31–46). In that challenging story, the disciples approach Jesus with a poignant question: Who will be saved? They want to know what the criteria for salvation and judgment will be. For ordinary Jews like Jesus and the disciples, the answers were rather clear. The Jews were God's chosen people. God had made a covenant with the Jews. God called them to a life of holiness which the people put into practice through the laws and rituals prescribed in the Torah. But Jesus did not respond in the usual, expected way. Instead he told a story.

All the people of the world are invited to assemble with God. And the criteria for membership in the assembly are not the laws and rituals prescribed in the Torah. They are far more expansive, inclusive, and challenging—feeding the hungry, giving drink to the thirsty, clothing the naked, caring for the sick and imprisoned. God's saving word transforms all that we have learned and come to know as the truth.

Assembly means fellowship and communion in the Lord Jesus Christ—a fellowship and communion that knows no bounds. Assembly means not family and friends, but a universal love for all who know the truth of nourishing hungry and thirsty people, caring for the sick and imprisoned, caring for people simply because they are people and have a need. The eucharistic assembly rejects the division caused by privilege, power, status, gender, race, age and ability, in favor of God's saving word, spoken to all who are willing to hear and take to heart the transforming power of God's love for us and our love for one another.

God's word saves us through the passover of Jesus Christ. Just as God saved the people of Israel through passover, bringing them from slavery in Egypt to freedom in the promised land, so God saves all people through the passover of Jesus Christ, inviting us to move from slavery to sin and selfishness to the freedom of life lived in love. God, in Jesus Christ, saves us through election, exodus, assembly, covenant and passover. God saves us through the liberating word spoken in Jesus Christ. God saves us through unconditional love—a love spoken through the word of Jesus, who is the word of God. God saves us as we assemble for eucharist, as we gather around the table of word and eucharist to give thanks that we are called to share our lives and offer ourselves in imitation of the Lord Jesus Christ, in selfless giving.

The Nature of Worship

When Christians gather for worship they are engaged in a formal, ritualistic pattern of response to God's invitation. While any Christian can pray and respond to God's invitation in a personal and even individualistic way, worship within the Christian context is an official, public, and communally sanctioned activity which relies on centuries-old rituals to express itself.[7] These communal rituals are the way Christians respond to God's invitation to conversion. Christians re-create the world mythologically, repeating ancient stories in ever-new contexts. All worship centers around remembering—remembering significant events of God's relationship with people in the past, because these events are still felt now to be extremely important, and because believers are convinced that the future must be directed by God's continuing activity and presence. In this sense, worship is repetitive or celebratory. It considers and reviews again and again God's love and goodness throughout the various seasons and cycles of our lives

Obviously, God is the object of such worship. God is experienced as both transcendent—wherein believers unite themselves to this powerful, revealing and mysterious source of love—and as immanent—wherein believers unite themselves to one another in a bond of fellowship and love which actually reflects the activity of God in their lives. The form of worship includes words, music, bodily movement and silent contemplation. The content of worship includes adoration, reverence, sorrow for one's sinfulness, gratitude and petition. Worship uses words or material objects that are seen as symbols (presence carriers), in that they either put us in touch with God through the meaning that is given to them, or they actually indicate for us the presence of God's love. For example, the water used in baptism is symbolic and worthy of veneration because we believe that it cleanses and purifies, and puts us in touch with the dying and rising of Jesus Christ. The bread and wine used in the eucharist are food for our journey and carriers of the presence of Christ as the personal embodiment of God's love.

Worship centers around major events in salvation history—primarily the life, passion, death, resurrection and glorification of Jesus Christ—and major events in the life of believers—primarily birth, membership in the community of faith, nourishment in the life of faith, restoration of broken relationships, and the recognition of our mortality. Christian worship has a twofold thrust or direction: it is oriented toward communion with God, and it works to unite individual worshippers as well as the whole community of faith. In the pastoral situation which begins this chapter, Bill begins this process by reconnecting with God and a significant member of the parish community. Worship fosters communion, fellowship and union with all the peoples of the world. Worship imposes an ethic upon us. If we are to be at all sincere in our worship, then we must live in accordance with the demand that our lives be motivated by love as God's life is. Christian worship has practical implications in that it compels us to work for the spread of God's kingdom of justice, love and peace in such ways as will be just and fair to all, bringing harmony and integrity not only to the community of faith but also to our environment and to all creation.[8]

The Sacramental Nature of Worship

In his writings and video presentations, Catholic theologian Father Richard McBrien has explored what he calls the "principle of sacramentality." If religion is generally defined as belief in and reverence for a supernatural power accepted as the creator and governor of the universe, and a specific unified system of this expression, then the Catholic sacraments are a unified system which expresses the relationship between God and believers. For Christians, God is the author of all that exists, and the world is the place where people can encounter God. Jesus Christ is a sacrament, a sign and personification of all that God is. Jesus is the paradigm, the instrument through which God encounters people. The church is also a sacrament—in all its activities, the church seeks to bring humanity to God. Christians believe that they are made in the image of God and through love they can be signs of the presence and saving activity of God through history. Through its rich and complex history the church has designated seven rituals through which it celebrates the saving activity of God—the initiation sacraments, baptism, confirmation and eucharist; the healing sacraments, reconciliation and the anointing of the sick and viaticum; and the commitment sacraments, marriage and orders.

Richard McBrien defines the seven sacraments at three different levels. At the first level, sacraments are any tangible, material reality in which God is present and through which God encounters people and people respond to God. And so, for example, a wedding ring, usually made of gold or silver, and sometimes including diamonds or other precious gems, is a common tangible and material object used in most cultures of the world. Within the Christian context of the sacrament of marriage, the wedding ring symbolizes the love without beginning or end of the couple entering into Christian marriage, which is a sign of the eternal love of God. Within the context of the sacrament of marriage, the couple pledges to imitate in their life of marriage the love without beginning or end of God, who is the author and creator of all life and love.

At the second level, sacraments are any reality or sign in the church that is useful for God's encounter with people. And so, for example, within the sacrament of baptism, water, oil, new white clothing and a lighted candle are essential components of the sacramental celebration. These material objects—water, oil, clothing and candle—are visible, material signs which communicate the new life which baptism implies. Baptism, in this specifically Christian context, is not simply a social ceremony of initiation into a community of faith, but a conscious and deliberate decision to live the new life of conversion, within the community of faith, to the Lord Jesus Christ. Baptism into the Catholic community means a new way of life, a special consecration as God's holy people, who pledge themselves to be the light of Jesus Christ in the world in which they live.

At the third level, sacraments are rituals, gestures or symbols which the church has explicitly designated to express its own reality, celebrate the saving activity of God and be the primary way by which members of the church can respond to God's presence, celebrate what God has done and cooperate with God in God's activity. One example is the Christian celebration of the eucharist, in which Christians ritualize, through gestures and symbols, their faith in God and their communion with one another and with the entire world. Christians are most naturally who they are in the celebration of the eucharist—an assembly of persons called together by God, nourished by the living word of God and the bread and wine of the eucharist, and missioned to the world in ministry and service to all those in need. The eucharist is the primary way by which the members of the church respond to God's presence, celebrate what God has done and participate with God in God's activity in the world.[9]

The *Catechism of the Catholic Church* describes sacraments in the following manner:

> Sacraments are "powers that come forth" from the Body of Christ (Cf. Lk 5:17; 6:19; 8:46), which is ever-living and life-giving. They are actions of the Holy Spirit at work in his Body, the Church. They are "the masterworks of God" in the new and everlasting covenant.[10]

This description relies on the insights of the fifth century pope and doctor of the church, Leo the Great. Sacraments are clearly rooted in the life and ministry of Jesus and entrusted to the church for the purpose of the ongoing conversion of people who profess faith in the God of Jesus Christ, who calls all people to new life. This description of the sacraments highlights the action of God's Spirit in the life of the community of faith.

Sacraments, then, are not so much objects of study as paradigms of initial and ongoing conversion in the life of the Christian community. Studying the sacraments, and understanding their origin, their historical developments throughout church history, their proper ritual celebration, is necessary and helpful. However, celebrating the sacraments within the community of faith and from the perspective of faith is equally necessary and helpful. It is only through worship from the perspective of a living faith that the sacraments make sense.

Catholic sociologist Father Andrew Greeley has articulated this uniquely Catholic understanding of sacraments in his notion of the "sacramental imagination."[11] Catholics imagine a God who is present in the world. For Catholics, the world is revelatory. As a result of sociological surveys of the U.S. population through several decades, Greeley finds that Catholics value experience, symbol and story, rather than creed, rite and institution. Catholics have a warm, affectionate, intimate and loving representation of God and a communitarian ethic which causes them to be tolerant of racial, ethnic and cultural diversity. Catholics assume a God who is present in the world, disclosing himself in and through creation—the world and all its events, objects and people tend, within this view, to be somewhat like God. Catholics value social relationships; equality over freedom; loyalty, obedience and patience.

Catholic sacraments are rooted in a unique understanding of God, and the relationship between God and the world. The sacraments celebrate the saving activity of God within the community of faith, which is always involved in both initial and ongoing conversion to the values of Jesus Christ.[12]

The Jewish Roots of Christian Worship

As a result of decades of research into Jesus of Nazareth and the origins and development of Christianity, it is now clear that the Catholic sacraments, though unique expressions of the worship of believers, have their roots in Judaism.[13] Jesus of Nazareth was a first-century Palestinian Jew. He looked like a Jew, talked like a Jew and worshipped like a Jew. His faith in God was nurtured within the context of a Jewish home and family, within the context of first-century Palestinian Judaism. Jesus of Nazareth knew the Jewish scriptures, proclaimed them in the local synagogues and reflected on them with anyone who would listen. When Jesus of Nazareth worshipped, he did so within the cycle of seasons and feasts kept by first-century Palestinian Jews. Jesus celebrated the annual Passover and the weekly Sabbath. He worshipped in local synagogues and at the Jerusalem temple, the center of Jewish worship. He knew the regulations of the Torah and the foundational stories which formed the basis of Jewish faith.

The annual round of synagogue and temple worship, and the various prayers and rituals surrounding family prayer and worship formed the basis of Jesus of Nazareth's understanding of God. Jesus used these various opportunities, especially his many fellowship meals with all kinds of people, to communicate his unique understanding of the relationship between God and both believers and nonbelievers alike. Christian worship has its basis in Jesus of Nazareth, who was proclaimed the Christ of faith by his many disciples and followers. The Christian "liturgy of the word" has clear roots in the weekly synagogue worship, and the Christian "liturgy of the eucharist" has clear roots in the weekly Sabbath meal, the annual Passover celebration, and the many other fellowship meals which Jesus celebrated. It is in this sense that Christian worship is rooted in Jewish worship. There is something very unique about Catholic worship in that it is centered on faith in the God of Jesus Christ. But there is something very Jewish about Catholic worship, in that there are many parallels and antecedents in the various forms of Jewish worship and prayer.

Many scholars point to the Roman destruction of the city of Jerusalem and the Jerusalem temple in 70 c.e. as a decisive event in the history of Jews and Christians. This political event seems to have been one of the motivating forces in the development of rabbinic Judaism, a Judaism dependent on the rabbis and local synagogues, and in the separation of Christianity from its Jewish roots. Between the death of Jesus and 70 c.e., many Jewish followers of Jesus saw themselves as a reform movement within Judaism, and many Gentile followers of Jesus saw themselves as members of a new religious tradition. The tension during this historical period is especially evident in the Acts of the Apostles and the synoptic gospels. After the destruction of the city of Jerusalem and the Jerusalem temple, the followers of Jesus identified themselves very clearly as Christians, followers of the God of Jesus Christ, and Jews identified themselves very clearly as Jews, followers of the God of Abraham and Moses. Understanding some of the history of the relationship and tension between Jews and the followers of Jesus enables us to appreciate the unique differences between two great religious communities, Jews and Christians, and understand the common roots of our two different ways of responding to God. As we explore the various sacramental celebrations of the Catholic Church in succeeding chapters, we will point out more of the Jewish roots of Christian worship.

Summary

Catholic sacraments have their foundation in the preaching and teaching ministry of Jesus Christ, a first-century Palestinian Jew. Understanding the theme of Jesus' preaching, the kingdom of God, and the radical call to conversion which membership in the kingdom implies, is critical to our understanding of Catholic worship. The Jewish roots of Christian worship and the specifically sacramental nature of Catholic worship enable us to see the various rituals, gestures and symbols designated by the church as celebrations of the saving activity of God in the church. Catholic sacraments function as paradigms of initial and ongoing conversion in the life of the community of faith.

Questions for Reflection and Discussion

1. Discuss your response to the notion that the kingdom of God is inclusive, transformative of the world, and a goal of invaluable worth. What does the image "kingdom of God" mean to you?

2. How does the Sunday eucharistic assembly demand a conversion of the individual and of the assembly itself?

3. Discuss your experiences of worship. Identify those experiences that tended to empower you. Identify those experiences that were not effective. What was missing?

4. Identify the material objects used in sacraments, i.e., water, oil, rings, etc. How are these valued in ordinary life? How does their religious use change our valuing of these things?

5. How do Catholics understand the relationship between God and humanity? Discuss some ways that this relationship is mediated through the sacraments.

THE SACRAMENTS
OF INITIATION

† † †

3

The *Rite of Christian Initiation of Adults*

*M*ark sat on the couch with the channel changer in his hand and newspapers on his chest. He did this every Sunday afternoon. Marcia sat at the dining room table near the window and was enjoying the autumn afternoon sun. She very much liked this time of day and this season. She was amused that Mark could watch two or three different football games and read the paper and do the crossword puzzle all at the same time.

Mark flipped through the channels over and over again. He then complained that he had broken his pencil. Marcia gave him another one. He shuffled through the paper, coming back every now and then to the crossword puzzle. He filled in a box or two and then began to look for something interesting on TV. While it was not unusual for Mark to be doing his Sunday afternoon rituals, he seemed to be particularly restless this afternoon.

"What's the matter, honey?" Marcia asked pleasantly.

"Nothing. I'm fine." Mark shuffled the papers again.

Marcia looked out the window at the trees with their full fall color and thought to herself about how wonderfully happy she was. The early months of her pregnancy were behind her. She was no longer uncomfortable. The doctors had assured her that she was very healthy and there was nothing to be worried about. She fantasized about playing in the falling leaves with her new baby in a year's time.

Mark grunted something about there not being any interesting games to watch and then asked Marcia if there was anything to eat. Marcia was a bit surprised because Mark was always concerned about his weight. He was paying more attention to his diet than usual because *he said he had to be in shape for the baby. They had been waiting for a baby for their six years of marriage. They were both very excited.*

"Don't we have any chips or pretzels?"

"No, Mark. Remember you told me not to keep that stuff in the house anymore? I have some cold cuts. Do you want a sandwich?"

Mark let out a big sigh and said, "No. I don't eat sandwiches in the middle of the afternoon." He repositioned himself on the couch and knocked all of the papers on the floor.

"That's it!" Marcia said as she got up from the table. "What's the matter with you this afternoon?"

"I don't know," Mark replied as he began to pick up the papers. Marcia helped him out and then asked him to come to the table with her. She led him by the hand to the chair nearest the window. The sun was casting a golden shower at the close of the day.

Mark began to laugh at himself. All at once he looked like the teenager Marcia had met so many years ago.

"Are you worried about the baby?" Marcia asked, while she still held his hand.

"Oh, no. It's not that. I feel great about the baby. Do you feel good about the baby?"

"Sure I do." Marcia drew him close to her and pushed the hair out of his eyes. "I've never seen you like this. You can't get comfortable. Are you worried about something? How can I help you if I don't know what's going on?"

Mark smiled. He loved her very deeply. He blushed a little and dropped his head. "You're going to think I'm silly," he said.

Marcia let go of his hand and sat straight up. "Tell me, please. What's going on?"

"Marcia, Marcia." Mark smiled while slowly saying her name. "This morning at church I met with Sister Christine. She said that we were ready to make the first big step in becoming Catholics. We are to participate in what they call a rite of election. It means that everyone will know that I am becoming a Catholic."

"Well, all our friends already know that you're becoming a Catholic and they think it's great. And it's going to happen around the same time as the baby comes." Marcia simply didn't understand.

Mark said: "We've talked about this for years. I knew I would want to become a Catholic when we had children. It makes a lot of sense to me. *I've enjoyed the classes much more than I expected to. I've learned an awful lot and I have found a lot of what they are teaching to be very inspiring. But the problem is...."* He sighed and got quiet.

Marcia was very patient and after a few minutes lifted his face with her hands and said, *"And the problem is...?"*

"The problem is that I have come to realize that I cannot become a Catholic for the baby. I can't become a Catholic even for you. I have got to become a Catholic for me. Don't you see?"

Marcia just looked at him and waited.

"If I become a Catholic, I am going to have to change. I am going to have to give up some ways of doing things that I have been doing all my life. I am going to have to be different and I'm not sure even how. But I know this much. If I stand up before everyone and say that I am really going to do this, then I'm really going to do it!"

Marcia smiled broadly. She stood up and kissed him on the forehead. She said: *"Every day you give me another reason to love you. I'll walk through this with you. We'll go one day at a time."*

Mark stood up and they embraced. They looked out the window to watch the dance of colored leaves.

Origins

For many Catholics, the *Rite of Christian Initiation of Adults (RCIA)* is something new, one of the many innovations which followed after the Second Vatican Council. The rite is actually something very old in the tradition of the church; it is a retrieval of the early church's ancient practice of initiating adults through a lengthy process of incorporation and inclusion into the community of faith. The rite is the initiation process for adults which culminates in baptism, confirmation and eucharist, usually celebrated at the annual Easter vigil. The rite is a fundamental pattern and paradigm of initial and ongoing conversion which not only initiates adults into the church but also enables them "to carry out the mission of the entire people of God in the church and in the world"[1] throughout the course of a lifetime.

The *Catechism of the Catholic Church* indicates that the sacraments of initiation—baptism, confirmation, and eucharist—lay the foundations of every Christian life. Quoting Pope Paul VI, the *Catechism* teaches:

> "The sharing in the divine nature given to men through the grace of Christ bears a certain likeness to the origin, development, and nourishing of natural life. The faithful are born anew by Baptism, strengthened by the sacrament of Confirmation, and receive in the Eucharist the food of eternal life. By means of these sacraments of Christian initiation, they thus receive in increasing measure the treasures of the divine life and advance toward the perfection of charity." (Paul VI, apostolic constitution, *Divinae consortium naturae:* AAS 63 [1971] 657; cf. RCIA Introduction 1–2)[2]

Adults who express a desire to belong to the Catholic Church are initiated into faith in the God of Jesus Christ. This initiation is a process, taking some time and involving conversion and catechesis. Initiation into the church is both an individual and a communal event, focusing on the interior conversion of those to be initiated, and on the evangelizing mission of the church itself. Adults initiated into the church become members of the body of Christ and, as such, are called to mission and ministry in the world. The Christian initiation process not only functions as a paradigm of initial and ongoing conversion for the unbaptized, but also for the community of faith, the baptized, who are called to a continual conversion of life. By taking an active role in the evangelizing mission of the church, the baptized are inspired and encouraged to renew again and again their own faith in the God of Jesus Christ.

Since baptism is initiation into the church of Jesus Christ, it is important to know how Jesus himself gathered followers and disciples. A look at the New Testament Gospels indicates that the primary relationship between Jesus and his followers was one of discipleship. Disciples are lifelong learners, persons who are able to be taught. Discipleship implies a lifelong commitment to following the example and the teachings of the master, Jesus Christ.

Jesuit theologian Father Thomas P. Rausch offers a helpful analysis of this important New Testament concept. The word "disciple" occurs more than 250 times in the gospels and Acts and most often refers to the followers of Jesus, who are co-workers with him sent to proclaim the coming of the kingdom of God. Rausch describes five unique characteristics of discipleship in relation to Jesus. First, the disciples of Jesus are chosen by him to be with him and to go out and preach. In Judaism, disciples chose their own master. Second, unlike Jewish rabbis who imposed restrictions on those qualified to be disciples, Jesus was rather inclusive in his call to discipleship, extending this relationship to tax collectors and sinners (Mk 2:15) and women (Lk 8:2). Third, Jesus' call to discipleship demands a radical religious conversion, which often meant leaving behind one's possessions (Mk 2:14; Mk 10:21; Lk 5:11; Lk 9:57–62; Lk 14:26). Fourth, discipleship means following Jesus by sharing his ministry of service and his life of poverty and itinerancy. And fifth, discipleship means a willingness to love others with a sacrificial love, which includes sharing with others, taking the last place, inclusivity, and bearing insult and injury. Discipleship in the New Testament means a personal following of Jesus that affects every dimension of human life.

> It shapes one's attitude toward property and wealth, affects a person's human and erotic relationships, gives a new meaning to love, changes the way one understands success and personal fulfillment, and, finally, calls one to enter into Jesus' paschal mystery.[3]

Many New Testament scholars indicate that Jesus of Nazareth desperately wanted to reform the religion of his day. Jesus was not alone in this desire for religious reform. John the Baptist is another example of a first-century Palestinian Jew who felt called by God to reform the Jewish faith. John called people to a baptism of repentance for the forgiveness of sins (Mk 1:4–5). John attracted many Jews of his day to participate in this baptism, including Jesus of Nazareth. Christian baptism was thus patterned after the baptism of Jesus by John. Jews of Jesus' day seem to have practiced at least two kinds of baptism: John's baptism of repentance for the forgiveness of sins; and proselyte baptism, whereby Gentiles were initiated into the Jewish faith. It is difficult to say whether or not Jesus actually baptized his own followers during his lifetime, yet Matthew's Gospel concludes with the following words:

> Go, therefore, and make disciples of all nations, baptizing
> them in the name of the Father, and of the Son, and of the
> holy Spirit, teaching them to observe all that I have com-
> manded you. And behold, I am with you always, until the
> end of the age. (Mt 28:19–20)

While the gospels leave us with a lot of unanswered questions
about the precise nature of baptism during the time of Jesus, it is
clear from Matthew's Gospel, and the rest of the New Testament
literature, that baptism was practiced by the followers of Jesus.
There has never really been a time in the church when there was
no baptism. The Acts of the Apostles tells us that the followers of
Jesus proclaimed the good news of Jesus Christ, invited people
to a conversion of heart, baptized with water, continued some
form of catechesis and shared fellowship in the Holy Spirit and
the eucharist (Acts 2:42).

Christian initiation is rooted in the life and ministry of Jesus
of Nazareth, and it implies conversion to the Lord Jesus Christ.
Christian initiation is patterned after the relationship of discipleship, a lifelong pattern of learning and conversion, living and
dying in imitation of Jesus Christ.

Historical Developments

The writings of the ancient church provide us with a little
more detail surrounding the practice of baptism. The *Didache,*
the *Apology* of Justin and Tertullian's *Apostolic Tradition,* dating
from the second and third century C.E., describe a process of
conversion and initiation, lasting some three years or more,
which includes evangelization, moral formation and gradual
inclusion of the candidates for baptism into the community of
faith.[4] Both the New Testament and other ancient church documents make clear that baptism was practiced by the followers of
Jesus as a means for including new members within the community of faith. Christian initiation was one, single but elaborate
ceremony which later generations of Christians would divide
into three separate sacramental celebrations. Thus, the gospels
and other writings of the ancient church indicate at least two

forms of baptism, a rather brief and simple form and a more elaborate and lengthy form, both practiced by the disciples and followers of Jesus.

What is clear from the New Testament and other ancient church documents is that Christian initiation was a decisive event in the lives of those who professed faith in the God of Jesus Christ. Candidates for baptism accepted Jesus Christ as the messiah, the one sent from God to save the world and to proclaim the kingdom of God. Candidates changed their allegiance—from former ways of life and worship to the way of life and worship professed by Jesus Christ. Candidates literally left aside their former ways of living to live as Jesus had taught. Christian initiation was a kind of new birth; candidates were initiated into a new way of life that brought them enlightenment and made them sharers in the life, passion, death and resurrection of Jesus Christ.

Christian initiation was not simply a social or cultural ceremony. While many of the customs and practices associated with baptism came from Jewish life and culture—for example, water baptism, anointings with oil, exorcisms, new clothes, lighted candles—Christian initiation involved professing the faith of Jesus Christ and belonging to a community of persons who lived and died, fasted and prayed after the example of Christ. Baptism was clearly a communal event. It was not simply incorporation into a community, but belonging to an evangelizing community of faith which sponsored, instructed, prayed and welcomed persons into the community. It is important to remember that another aspect of the decisive nature of Christian initiation is the fact that Christians were not well respected during the first three centuries after the death of Jesus. Many of the followers of Jesus Christ and those they baptized were persecuted and executed for their faith. Those who came forward for Christian initiation knew that they risked their very lives for the sake of their faith.

The church's current *Rite of Christian Initiation of Adults* is clearly a retrieval of ancient baptismal practice, as found in the New Testament and other ancient church documents. The followers of Jesus took his command to make disciples of all the nations (Mt 28:19) quite seriously. While the process of Christian initiation was at first quite simple, as successive generations of

Christians moved into various cultures and lands, and as the church grew from a few hundred to thousands of members spread throughout the ancient world, the process became more elaborate and formalized.

In the early centuries of the church, baptism was celebrated only at Easter and usually by the bishop. Candidates for baptism were enrolled in the catechumenate, and the period of probation and instruction lasted for several years. During this time, Christians instructed candidates in the faith and helped them discern how to live as the gospel required. This often meant a change of occupation. Christians could not engage in making idols or work in the circus or the military because at this time these occupations were viewed as inconsistent with the message and mission of Jesus Christ. They had to demonstrate by their everyday habits that they had, in fact, made decisive changes in their lives. They were to turn away from sin—especially public and scandalous acts, such as murder, adultery and apostasy, and from their former ways of worship. The catechumens could not worship with the Christians until they had clearly demonstrated a sincere and genuine desire to belong to the community of faith. Because Christians were considered to be subversives in the Roman empire, there was always the danger that some might infiltrate the community of faith for the purpose of destroying it. Once the members of the community were satisfied that the catechumens' conversion was genuine, they were admitted to the community through baptism, confirmation and eucharist. Now they were Christians, but the process of their formation was by no means complete. In the days and weeks following Easter, the newly baptized were instructed further in the mysteries of the faith they had celebrated—mystagogical catechesis. During this period of postbaptismal catechesis, the newly baptized were more clearly included in the life and worship of the community and instructed in how they themselves could take up the mission and ministry of the church. It was during this time that the newly baptized began to learn the "mysteries of the faith." Prebaptismal catechesis focused on the process of conversion to faith in the God of Jesus Christ. This was the essential result of the lengthy process leading up to Christian initiation. Postbaptismal catechesis focused on learning the particulars of Christian faith—the sacraments, the scriptures, morality and spirituality. During this catechesis the newly baptized were gradually incorporated and included in the daily life of the community of faith.

A major change in baptismal practice occurred during the fourth century, when the Roman emperor Constantine converted to Christianity in 313 C.E. In 380 C.E. Christianity was proclaimed the official religion of the Roman empire. It was now no longer necessary to fear persecution and Christians began to worship rather publicly. During the fourth and fifth centuries large numbers of people came forward for Christian initiation. The problem, however, was that many people joined the church because it was fashionable to be a Christian. The previous emphasis on conversion lost some of its vigor as people realized that becoming Christian now meant protection and favor by the Roman government. Being Christian no longer meant being all that different or separating oneself from society. Baptism lost a great deal of its radical decisiveness, elitism and martyrdom. Following the understanding of baptism contained in the New Testament and the writings of the fathers of the church, baptism was understood to be "for the forgiveness of sins." As yet there was no clear understanding of what to do when baptized Christians sinned. Since the sacrament of reconciliation had not yet developed, baptism was a once-in-a-lifetime opportunity for the forgiveness of sins. Thus, so many converts to Christianity became catechumens, but delayed their baptism until they were near death so that they could die with all their sins forgiven. Some of the fathers of the church, like Tertullian, began to articulate a new rationale for baptism. Those who were baptized into the Christian community were to live in this world and penetrate it with the mission of Christ. Baptism was not so much the "once-in-a-lifetime" remission of sins but the beginning of a life in Christ, a lifelong process of conversion and reconciliation.

As more and more people were initiated into the church, especially during the fourth and fifth centuries, the catechumenate began to disappear, probably because most people were now baptized. By the Middle Ages it really no longer existed. As we will see in the next chapter on baptism, adult Christian initiation and the beginnings of the practice of infant baptism meant that by this time in history most adults were already baptized and so there was no longer any need to concentrate on adult initiation. And so from the Middle Ages up to the middle of the twentieth century, infant baptism became the normative practice within the church.

Several developments during the twentieth century prepared the way for the retrieval of the ancient church's practice of adult initiation. Catholics learned that many other Christians did not baptize infants. This led both Catholic and Christian theologians to reexamine the scriptural and historical data more thoroughly. This research and dialogue led most Christian scholars to admit that both adult and infant baptism were practiced in the early church. Scholars discovered that there was no consistent baptismal practice in the history of the church. Some infants were merely baptized; other infants were baptized, confirmed and eucharistized. Some adults were admitted to the catechumenate and remained catechumens for most of their lives; other adults, after a several-year period of catechesis, were baptized, confirmed and eucharistized at the annual Easter vigil. Throughout history, baptism of both adults and infants took place, sometimes only at specified times during the year, and at other times in history they were celebrated frequently throughout the year. As the Second Vatican Council was beginning, most of what we now know of the history of Christian initiation was presented to the bishops, with the request that the council restore the ancient practice of adult baptisms—the *Rite of Christian Initiation of Adults.* After the council the *Rite for Infant Baptism* was revised in 1969 and the *Rite of Christian Initiation of Adults* was published in the United States in 1988.

The diversity of initiation practice within Christianity is explained in the *Catechism of the Catholic Church,* nos. 1230–1233. In the early centuries Christian initiation developed rapidly to accommodate the large number of persons seeking baptism. A long period of catechumenate, including several liturgical celebrations, culminated in the celebration of the sacraments of initiation. As infant baptism became the norm, the catechumenate disappeared and a postbaptismal catechumenate developed to nurture the faith of growing infants and children. The Second Vatican Council restored for the Latin church the ancient practice of the catechumenate for adults seeking baptism. The process and rites for this are found in the *Rite of Christian Initiation for Adults (RCIA)*.

This brief review of some of the historical developments in Christian initiation practice reveals that our earliest historical records describe baptism as an elaborate rite for adults which includes three sacraments—baptism, confirmation and the eucharist. In this earliest stage of Christian initiation, there was a great emphasis on conversion and the community aspects of initiation. The community sponsored the candidates, instructed them, prayed for them and assembled to welcome them after baptism. Christian initiation implied for the newly baptized an active role in the life of the community and a decisive change in lifestyle. The earliest historical records also indicate that infants were routinely brought to the church for Christian initiation—some for baptism, others for baptism, confirmation and the eucharist. Here we have the beginnings, quite early on, of the separation of the sacraments of initiation into three stages, spread over many years. As the *Catechism of the Catholic Church* points out, throughout this history of Christian initiation cultural customs were always included in the church's rites of initiation—water, oil, new clothes, lighted candles, etc. Christian initiation means many things to many different people, reflecting the cultural and theological pluralism of various eras of history. As Catholic theologian Joseph Martos has concluded:

> At least we can say that baptism remains a door to the sacred for most Catholics because it is still a ritual through which they enter a religious society which stands for a sacred meaning of life and which opens the way to experiences of the sacred in childhood, adolescence, and adulthood. For parents and others who attend baptismal ceremonies the ritual can in addition disclose dimensions of their religious beliefs which are sometimes obscured, and can deepen their commitment to what they discover through their participation in it. And for those who reflect

on the action of baptism and, like Paul of Tarsus, ask what it
means, it can be a symbolic representation of the central
mystery of Christianity.[5]

The evolution of baptismal practice witnesses to the mystery of
God's love for us and our love for one another, throughout the
course of our entire lives.

Theology and Celebration of the Rite

St. Paul was the first to provide us with a theology of baptism. In the early fifties C.E., Paul writes to the Corinthians that
"in one Spirit we were all baptized into one body, whether Jews
or Greeks, slaves or free" (1 Cor 12:13). Salvation comes
through the death and resurrection of Christ. Even though baptism is for the remission of sins, it is also a turning to Christ, a
decisive beginning of a new life in Christ, a life of discipleship—
lifelong learning of the ways of Jesus and lifelong conversion to
the God of Jesus Christ. For Paul, baptism incorporates us into
the death, burial and resurrection of Christ (Col 2:12; Eph
2:1–6; Phil 3:10–11), and into the body of Christ (1 Cor
12:12–14, 27). Baptism purifies (Eph 5:26), cleansing our
hearts from an evil conscience (Heb 10:22). We become "dead
to sin and living for God in Christ Jesus" (Rom 6:11). Baptism
requires that we live "not under law but under grace" (Rom
6:12–23). For Paul, Christian initiation is a process of total
identification with Christ.

Baptism incorporates people into the church, associates
them with the death and resurrection of Christ, effects a forgiveness of sins, and orients people to the worship of God and the
wider mission of the church. Baptism is thus not an individual
event, but a communal event. We are an initiating community
which models itself on Jesus Christ, who identified himself with
sinful humanity and worked to redeem sinful humanity. Baptism
calls us to mission, the mission of Jesus Christ.

The *Rite of Christian Initiation of Adults* describes the theology of Christian initiation in the following four "periods" and
three "steps":

Period of Evangelization and Precatechumenate
> This is a time, of no fixed duration or structure, for inquiry and introduction to gospel values, an opportunity for the beginning of faith.

First Step: Acceptance into the Order of Catechumens
> This is the liturgical rite, usually celebrated on some annual date or dates, marking the beginning of the catechumenate proper, as the candidates express and the church accepts their intention to respond to God's call to follow the way of Christ.

Period of the Catechumenate
> This is the time, in duration corresponding to the progress of the individual, for the nurturing and growth of the catechumens' faith and conversion to God; celebrations of the word and prayers of exorcism and blessing are meant to assist the process.

Second Step: Election or Enrollment of Names
> This is the liturgical rite, usually celebrated on the first Sunday of Lent, by which the church formally ratifies the catechumens' readiness for the sacraments of initiation and the catechumens, now the elect, express the will to receive these sacraments.

Period of Purification and Enlightenment
> This is the time immediately preceding the elect's initiation, usually the Lenten season preceding the celebration of this initiation at the Easter vigil; it is a time of reflection, intensely centered on conversion, marked by celebration of the scrutinies and presentations and of the preparation rites on Holy Saturday.

Third Step: Celebration of the Sacraments of Initiation
> This is the liturgical rite, usually integrated into the Easter vigil, by which the elect are initiated through baptism, confirmation, and the eucharist.

Period of Postbaptismal Catechesis or Mystagogy
> This is the time, usually the Easter season, following the celebration of initiation, during which the newly initiated

experience being fully a part of the Christian community by means of pertinent catechesis and particularly by participation with all the faithful in the Sunday eucharistic celebration.[6]

This brief overview of the various periods and steps in the *Rite of Christian Initiation of Adults* reveals the rich theology of Christian initiation and the many assumptions about church which the rite implies.

The *Rite of Christian Initiation of Adults* assumes that the local church will be an evangelizing community. As the church assembles to worship, it realizes its mission to the world and proclaims the values of the gospel to all the world. Christian initiation is both an individual and a communal process. Central to the belief of Christians is the fact that God speaks to us all and invites all people into the community of faith. The baptized recognize their mission to the world to announce the good news of Jesus Christ by inviting others to consider these values and this faith as addressed to them. An evangelizing community is always on the lookout for opportunities to bring the Christian faith to those who express a desire to learn about the God of Jesus Christ.

Our human experience teaches us that most of us look for some meaning and value in life beyond that which is readily available. We search for love, commitment, and making a difference in the world in which we live. We hunger for those sacred moments which enrich our lives and lead us to the fullest realization of what it means to be human. An evangelizing community of faith is able to make the connection between human experience and sacred experience. An evangelizing community of faith is able to see how the gospel values meet the human need for love, commitment, and making a difference in the world in which we live. Many who come to the church seeking Christian initiation come because they are without hope or are in need of healing; others come simply because they are married to a Catholic and want a source of unity in their family; still others come from other religious traditions which have left them unsatisfied. The period of evangelization and precatechumenate is an opportunity for all of the baptized to go beyond their own personal faith to a kind of universalizing faith where the gospel of Jesus Christ becomes the way to introduce others into the community of faith. Parish communities are challenged to present the gospel to others in an attempt to show how this message fills the void in their lives. This process leads to the first step, acceptance into the order of catechumens, where people express their desire to respond to God's invitation to faith, and the community accepts the responsibility to nurture them in the faith.

Conversion is central to Christian initiation. Fundamental to the process is the acknowledgement that each of us comes to faith in our own way and in our own time. With the prayer and support of other Christians and friends, we gradually begin to review the process of our life journey and grow in our understanding of what it means to profess faith in the God of Jesus Christ. Faith is not merely an individual, private gift of God, but a call from the community of faith to the hard and sometimes difficult process of turning our lives around. We are nurtured in faith by people of faith. We begin to see, within the context of a nurturing and supportive community, that we are called beyond ourselves. We are brought to full humanity only in relationship with others. God calls us to faith through the word of God. Here, we are invited to reflect on the great themes of scripture; to prayer, which develops our relationship with ourselves, others and God; to blessing, which enables us to be thankful for all of the gifts which only come from God. This process leads quite naturally to the liturgical rite of election, where catechumens declare their readiness for the sacraments of initiation.

During the period of purification and enlightenment, the candidates for Christian initiation are finally prepared. During these weeks, candidates reflect on the Lenten scriptures and their call to conversion, and celebrate the scrutinies, rites for self-searching and repentance. These rites are meant to help the candidates understand their human weakness, and to strengthen their resolve to accept Christ, who is the way, the truth and the life. During this time, the candidates are presented with the creed and the Lord's Prayer, because these express the heart of the church's faith and prayer. This final preparation brings the candidates to the celebration of the sacraments of Christian initiation—baptism, confirmation and eucharist—at the annual Easter vigil.

During the final period of postbaptismal catechesis or myst-agogy, the newly baptized are incorporated as full members of the community of faith and gradually nurtured into the life and mission of the church. Through regular participation in Sunday eucharist and continued catechesis, the newly baptized are intro-duced to the full range of Catholic faith and belief, and chal-lenged to live the ethical and moral demands of the gospel in their daily living.

The *Catechism of the Catholic Church* makes it clear that the theology of baptism is contained in the rites, gestures and words of its celebration. The sign of the cross at the beginning of the celebration is the mark of belonging to Christ and the sign of our redemption through Christ's death. The proclamation of the word of God enlightens candidates and the baptized as they travel in faith along the lifelong journey of conversion and repen-tance. The scrutinies and exorcisms, the anointing with the oil of catechumens and the laying on of hands prepare the candidates for liberation from sin and a lifelong rejection of evil. The bap-tismal water, consecrated by the Holy Spirit of God at the Easter vigil, signifies that those who will be baptized will be born again through water and the Holy Spirit. The actual water baptism, either through a triple immersion or a triple pouring, transforms the candidates into baptized members of the community of faith. Through water and the Holy Spirit they die to sin and rise with Christ to new life. The anointing with sacred chrism, perfumed oil consecrated by the bishop, signifies the gift of the spirit to the newly baptized who, like Christ, are anointed priest, prophet and king. As priest they offer sacrifices of praise and thanksgiving to God; as prophet they announce the good news of Jesus Christ in their own time and place; as king they serve the needs of all the world. The white garment symbolizes that the baptized have become a new creation and have put on Christ. The candle, lit from the Easter candle, signifies that through baptism they have become, like Christ, the light of the world. And finally, baptized and sealed with the gift of the Holy Spirit, they are welcomed for the first time to the eucharist, where they begin their new life, in union with the entire community of faith.[7]

We can see in the *Rite of Christian Initiation of Adults* the full and diverse range of theology associated with Christian initiation. Baptism is new life in Christ, a conversion to the God of Jesus Christ and the gospel values. Baptism cleanses, purifies, enlightens, forgives sins, initiates people into the community of faith and introduces people to a lifelong journey of conversion. Through gestures, words and symbols, the rite witnesses to the mystery of God and the mystery of life, lived in imitation of the Lord Jesus Christ.

Pastoral Challenges

The *Rite of Christian Initiation of Adults* is still relatively new for all of us. The first pastoral challenge is familiarity and understanding of the rationale, theology, structure and use of the rite. Like all aspects of the church's worship, the *Rite of Christian Initiation of Adults* requires careful study and analysis. For many persons engaged in pastoral ministry, this is a challenge. The newness of the rite prevents it from having a part of the mind and heart of Catholics who gather for worship on a regular basis. Experience teaches us that only over time, and with careful, thoughtful and prayerful use do the rites of the church become regular patterns of worship in the life of the community of faith. As pastoral ministers engage in study and understanding of the rite, and gain confidence in celebrating the rite with the worshipping community, it will become a more integral part of Catholic life and worship.

A second challenge of the *Rite of Christian Initiation of Adults* is understanding that no single process of Christian initiation will meet the diverse needs of those who express a desire to become Catholic. As we have previously mentioned, persons who come to the church seeking Christian initiation come for a variety of reasons, from a variety of backgrounds, and at various stages in their lives. Persons already familiar with the Catholic Church have different needs than those who have no familiarity at all. Persons in their twenties have different needs from persons in their sixties. People who have already experienced a significant religious conversion have different needs from those who are just beginning to search for love and commitment, and trying to make a difference in the world. These are but a few of the exceptional circumstances which need to be taken into account in the rite. While the *Rite of Christian Initiation of Adults* is mandatory in the United States, the *General Introduction,* numbers 34 and 35, clearly urges ministers to take "into account the existing circumstances and others' needs, as well as the wishes of the faithful" in adapting the rite to special circumstances and to use the various options allowed within the rite.

The third and most critical challenge of the *Rite of Christian Initiation of Adults* is the fact that it implies and requires an evangelizing community of faith. Since the Second Vatican Council, Catholics are in the process of renewing their understanding of themselves as a community called to faith and mission in the world. We are called, not simply to a personal and individualized faith in the God of Jesus Christ, but to a universalizing faith which compels us to announce the good news of Jesus Christ by inviting others to consider membership in the community of faith as the path to salvation. This requires that the local parish community has the ability and willingness to share their own stories of coming to faith so that candidates for Christian initiation can be nurtured and supported in their own journey of faith. This is an especially critical challenge in the United States, where religion is often considered a private and personal affair. Catholic parishes that have used the rite have found, however, that the evangelizing mission of the church, once recognized, understood and practiced by the local community, is not only one of the best ways to renew the life of the baptized, but also one of the best ways to follow the command of Jesus to "go, therefore, and make disciples of all nations." (Mt 28:19)

Summary

The *Rite of Christian Initiation of Adults* is a retrieval of the church's ancient practice of Christian initiation, which is a fundamental pattern and paradigm of initiation and ongoing conversion.

There has never really been a time in the church when there was no baptism. Through the various stages of the rite, a process taking some time and involving conversion, catechesis and support from the community of faith, adults are initiated into faith through baptism, confirmation and the eucharist. Rooted in the ministry of Jesus and the practice of the ancient church, the *Rite of Christian Initiation of Adults* incorporates people into the church, through the proclamation of the good news of Jesus Christ, the invitation to a conversion of heart, baptism with water, continued catechesis and shared fellowship in the Holy Spirit and the eucharist.

Questions for Reflection and Discussion

1. Share your experiences of becoming part of a new group or community. What was it like to start a new job, move to a new town, begin a new school? How were you made to feel welcome or unwelcome? What did you have to do to get a sense of belonging?

2. Many times in the past we described a person who changed religious denominations as a "convert." In this chapter the word "conversion" means something more. How do you understand "convert" and "conversion" now?

3. Identify some of the steps for inclusion into the worshipping community. How do you feel about separating the "catechumens" from those who have been fully initiated?

4. What are some of the qualities of an "evangelizing" community?

5. Why would the Christian initiation process be good for your parish?

4

Baptism

*S*arah took the baby in her arms and sat down in the rocker with a great deal of pleasure. It was a wonderful rocker. It creaked and rolled with her, and the sounds comforted her like an old friend. The baby looked up at her, and with a lovely yawn, gently fell off to sleep.

Sarah rocked the baby and hummed a lullaby tune that sprang from the love in her heart. She knew the tune but was not sure anyone else knew it. It was a lullaby that had been born of sitting in this same rocker, rocking the children of her youth. It was the private song of a mother to a child that no one else really needed to know.

Sarah simply enjoyed the moment. It had been such a full and wonderful day. She, who would normally be in the kitchen organizing things, or out visiting, was quite content to leave all of that business to others, and claimed these precious moments with this baby all to herself. Back and forth she rocked, matching the rhythms of the innocent child's breathing. What could be better than this? With her humming and rocking, Sarah made herself and the baby so comfortable that the noise of the departing guests could be pleasantly ignored.

Sarah remembered the day that her husband had brought this old rocker home. It had been such a big purchase for him. Things were tight in those days, and most luxuries had to be avoided. But this rocker was a gift of his love for her. He bought it on a payment plan he really couldn't afford, but took the risk because he wanted her to know that he would be part of the difficult days of her pregnancy and the early days of raising their children. Sometimes it's just good to keep some old things around. She had comforted, fed and nourished five newborn babies in this chair, but rarely had a moment of rocking been so satisfying for her.

Sarah shifted her weight and rearranged the baby to get a little more comfortable. As she pulled the baby close to herself, she noticed a peculiar smell on the crown of the baby's head. "What is this?" she

54

thought as she drew closer for inspection. There was a strange odor, not like any shampoo or lotion for babies that she knew of. This was like a spice from the orient. What could it be? Yes. It was the oil of baptism.

    Sarah began to remember the ceremony. There were many babies. Sarah was sure that no baby was more wanted or loved than the baby she held in her arms. This granddaughter was her first. She had been waiting for a very long time for this child. Her son and his wife discovered shortly after marriage that they would not be able to have children of their own. They had only envisioned their marriage as one with children. On the day the doctor had told them of their situation, they began the long process of adoption.

    The adoption process had been filled with a great deal of emotion. Sarah's son had been most cooperative, even to the point of denying his deep disappointment of their situation. There had been many promises made to the couple over the years about when and what type of child might be available to them. There was one occasion when the adoption agency had promised the young couple that a child would be born and ready for them in one week. There was so much excitement and preparations made. Sarah brought her wonderful well-used rocker as a gift to the expectant parents. The birth mother had changed her mind on the day after the birth. The grief in the house was profound. The only way Sarah could comfort her son was to insist that they keep the rocker for another day. Another day and another child had come.

    There had been so much cautious expectation over this chosen child that Sarah listened to the words of baptism more carefully than before. She heard something that she had not remembered, although she was sure it had been said over her own five children. The priest said at the very beginning over the child, "I claim you for Christ our Savior by the sign of the cross." She knew how much her son and daughter-in-law wanted this child, how they claimed it for their own. Now there were new words said. "I claim you for Christ our Savior."

    The baby began to stir, and Sarah called to the mother: "It's time for you to take your Julie." As she got up out of the old rocker and passed the baby to her mother, Sarah resolved that she would do everything a grandmother could do to raise a child that was chosen, loved and claimed for Christ.

Origins

As we indicated in the previous chapter on the *Rite of Christian Initiation of Adults*, baptism has its origins in the New Testament notion of discipleship. Jesus called people to discipleship—a lifelong relationship, a lifelong commitment to following the example and the teachings of the master, Jesus Christ. It is clear from the New Testament that baptism was practiced by the followers of Jesus. Baptism is both an individual and a communal event. Baptism requires a conversion of heart to the values, attitudes and beliefs of Jesus Christ, and incorporation into a community of faith which, through word, worship, witness and service, continues to work for the commonwealth of justice and peace which Jesus inaugurated through his preaching of the kingdom of God. While there is no specific mention of the practice of baptizing infants in the New Testament, the *Catechism of the Catholic Church* summarizes the importance of infant baptism in the following way:

> The practice of infant Baptism is an immemorial tradition of the Church. There is explicit testimony to this practice from the second century on, and it is quite possible that, from the beginning of the apostolic preaching, when whole "households" received baptism, infants may also have been baptized. (Cf. *Acts* 16:15, 33; 18:8; *1 Cor* 1:16; CDF, instruction, *Pastoralis actio:* AAS 72 [1980] 1137–1156)[1]

However, while infant baptism is clearly an essential part of the tradition of the church, the obvious critical issue is the nature of discipleship for infants, who are incapable of making lifelong commitments.

Historical Developments

Infant baptism began early in the history of the church. Christians probably acted from a very natural instinct in baptizing infants and left it to others to justify their actions later. Among the many testimonies to infant baptism is the following from Hippolytus in 215:

> When they come to the water, let the water be pure and

> flowing. And they shall put off their clothes. And they shall
> baptize the little children first. And if they can answer for
> themselves, let them answer. But if they cannot, let their par-
> ents answer or someone from their family.[2]

This rather simple reference to the baptism of infants in the third
century is the beginning of a gradually increasing practice of infant
baptism. Eventually, by the fifth century, the baptism of infants
became the norm in the church. There was, perhaps, a rather simple reason for the inclusion of children in baptism. The early Christians were convinced of the message of Jesus and continued to
preach that message to anyone who would listen, even at the risk of
persecution and death. As entire families came forward for Christian baptism, they included their entire households. Parents quite
naturally want to pass on good things to their children, even
though the children may not understand what is being passed on to
them. Such was probably the case in the early centuries of the
church. Adults coming forward for baptism promised a lifelong
commitment of conversion and membership in the community of
faith. They brought their children forward for baptism because
they wanted them to be nurtured in the life of conversion to the
Lord Jesus Christ and in the life of the Christian community.

There were many other reasons for the rise of the practice
of infant baptism. As early Christians read and interpreted the
New Testament, they understood baptism to be necessary for salvation. They saw baptism in the church of Jesus Christ as the
path to life forever in the kingdom of God. Additionally, there
was a high infant mortality rate during this time in history, and
thus the necessity to be baptized as early as possible so that children could be assured of salvation.

Augustine of Hippo (354–430) provided the church with a
rationale for infant baptism which still endures today. He coined
the term "original sin"—referring to the sin of Adam and Eve,
and to the universality of that sin throughout all of history.
Augustine developed his theology of original sin in reaction to
Pelagius (350–425), a teacher in Rome, who taught that infants
are not born with any proclivity to sin, and so there is no necessity for baptism since there are no sins to be forgiven an infant.

Augustine, however, believed that the sin of Adam and Eve is passed on through procreation, from parents to children. Augustine identified as evidence of original sin the human tendency to yearn for self-gratification. According to Augustine, therefore, infant baptism was necessary for salvation. Through baptism the infant was oriented toward the good, toward God, rather than toward evil and self-gratification. This teaching on original sin is confirmed and summarized in the *Catechism of the Catholic Church,* no. 1250. For Augustine, then, infant baptism was the path to salvation, removing the original sin of infants and bringing them into a state of grace.

As the practice of infant baptism spread through the church, the obvious problem was how to ensure that children baptized as infants grew in discipleship. Remember that in the case of adults there was a lengthy period, lasting as long as three years, during which they were instructed and nurtured in the faith, both prior to and after their initiation. An infant cannot profess the faith, cannot make a pledge of allegiance to Jesus Christ, cannot understand what it means to live a life of conversion as a member of the community of faith. Infants are not capable of participating in any kind of catechesis to prepare them for baptism. It was this fact which prompted some of the reformers during the Protestant Reformation to deny the value of infant baptism. In response to this varied practice of infant baptism on the part of the reformers, the Council of Trent strongly reaffirmed the baptism of infants and the need for catechesis as infants grew through childhood, adolescence and adulthood.

In the years prior to Vatican II, much research on Christian initiation occurred, so that when Vatican II actually began, there was strong interest in retrieving the *Rite of Christian Initiation of Adults* and in revising the *Rite for the Baptism of Children.* In 1969 the revised *Rite for the Baptism of Children* was published, and it clearly emphasizes the critical role of parents and godparents in passing on the faith of the church to children. The parents of children up to the age of reason and discretion are instructed in the faith through a baptismal preparation program, since it is the parents who will be the first teachers of the faith to the children. This catechesis continues as parish communities provide sacramental preparation programs for first reconciliation, first communion and confirmation. The rise in the practice of infant baptism is one reason for the separation of the sacraments of initiation—infants are baptized and children are eucharistized and confirmed at various times during the elementary and high school years. Children who have reached the age of reason and discretion participate in a form of the *Rite of Christian Initiation of Adults,* in which they are catechized and then receive the three sacraments of initiation.

While the early history of baptism for adults centered around the annual celebration of Lent and Easter, the rise in the practice of infant baptism has placed the liturgical celebration often to within weeks of the infant's birth. Thus, baptism is typically celebrated in many parishes on a monthly basis.

Theology and Celebration of the Rite

Baptism incorporates people into the church, joins them with the death and resurrection of Christ, effects a forgiveness of sins, and orients people to the worship of God and the wider mission of the church. Baptism is thus not an individual event, but a communal event. We are initiated into a community of faith which models itself on Jesus Christ, who identified himself with sinful humanity and worked to redeem sinful humanity. Baptism calls us to mission, the mission of Jesus Christ.

In the case of the baptism of infants, it is clear that the parents are bringing their infants to the church for baptism because they intend to pass on the faith to their infants within the context of the local community of faith. Parents, godparents and the local community of faith take on a serious responsibility at the time of infant baptism. As the rite indicates:

> To fulfill the true meaning of the sacrament, children must later be formed in the faith in which they have been baptized. The foundation of this formation will be the sacrament itself, which they have already received. Christian formation, which is their due, seeks to lead them gradually to learn God's plan in Christ, so that they may ultimately accept for themselves the faith in which they have been baptized.[3]

Infant baptism typically begins with a parish preparation program for the parents and godparents of the infant to be baptized. While the timing and duration of these preparation programs vary from parish to parish, essentially the program seeks to elicit from parents and godparents their understanding of the sacraments of initiation and the role of parents, godparents, family, friends and the community of faith in their duties and responsibilities of nurturing infants and children in the faith. A wide variety of catechetical materials have been developed to assist parents in passing on the faith to their children.

The rite begins with a reception of the children in which the parents name their child and state their intention to have their child baptized in the church of Jesus Christ. The presider then informs the parents of their responsibility for bringing up the child in the faith. The presider then verifies the willingness of the godparents to assist the parents in their work of nurturing the child in the faith. All present then trace the sign of the cross on the forehead of the child.

The rite then proceeds to a celebration of the word of God, which includes readings from the scriptures, a homily, prayers of the faithful, a prayer of exorcism and anointing with the oil of catechumens. This part of the rite clearly indicates that baptism is oriented toward Jesus Christ, and focuses upon the conversion required of those who claim to be his followers. Baptism orients people to a lifelong commitment, a lifelong relationship to Jesus Christ and his teachings. Parents and godparents will be the first teachers of the child, the first to proclaim the word of God to their children. The prayer of exorcism expresses the Christian community's desire to protect the children from the forces of evil and sin in the world and, with the grace of God and the power of Christ's death, to bring the children to walk, not in darkness but in the light of Jesus Christ. The children are then anointed on the breast with the oil of catechumens, which marks them as belonging to God.

The rite then proceeds to the celebration of the sacrament of baptism. At this time all present move to the baptismal font where the water is blessed. After this, the presider leads the parents, godparents and all others present in a renunciation of sin and profession of faith. In the words of the rite:

Dear parents and godparents:
You have come here to present these children for baptism.
By water and the Holy Spirit they are to receive the gift of
new life from God, who is love. On your part, you must
make it your constant care to bring them up in the practice
of the faith. See that the divine life which God gives them is
kept safe from the poison of sin, to grow always stronger in
their hearts. If your faith makes you ready to accept this
responsibility, renew now the vows of your own baptism.
Reject sin; profess your faith in Christ Jesus. This is the faith
of the Church. This is the faith in which these children are
about to be baptized.[4]

This instruction makes clear that infant baptism is the beginning
of a long process of initiation into the faith of Jesus Christ and
that the primary teachers of the faith are parents, godparents
and the community of faith.

The children are then baptized, anointed with chrism,
clothed with a white garment and given a candle lighted from
the Easter candle. Water, oil, white clothing and candle are all
important symbols of the new life which baptism implies of
those who profess faith in the Lord Jesus Christ. This section of
the rite concludes with a special prayer over the ears and mouths
of the children:

The Lord Jesus made the deaf hear and the dumb speak.
May he soon touch your ears to receive his word, and your
mouth to proclaim his faith, to the praise and glory of God
the Father.[5]

The rite then concludes with the Lord's Prayer and a special
blessing for the mothers, the fathers, and all those present for
the baptism. The presider's introduction to this final part of the
rite is clear about the theology of infant baptism:

Dearly beloved, these children have been reborn in baptism.
They are now called children of God, for so indeed they are.
In confirmation they will receive the fullness of God's Spirit.
In holy communion they will share the banquet of Christ's
sacrifice, calling God their Father in the midst of the Church.

In their name, in the Spirit of our common sonship, let us
pray together in the words our Lord has given us.[6]

Infant baptism is clearly a beginning, an initiation into the faith
of Jesus Christ, which is completed in confirmation and
eucharist. Infant baptism relies on parents, godparents and the
community of faith to take an active part in the ritual of infant
baptism and in nurturing children in the faith. Infant baptism is
about parents and godparents assuming their roles as the first
teachers of their children in all things, especially the faith. The
baptism of children presumes continued attention to the sharing
of faith experiences and religious education as the children grow
and mature.

Pastoral Challenges

Commonsense experience teaches us that parents want to
hand on good things to their children, even though the children
may not understand what is being passed on to them. Early
Christians brought their entire households forward for Christian
initiation, including their children, because they wanted them to
be an integral part of the community of faith. Infant baptism has
always been, therefore, the beginning of a lifelong process of
conversion and commitment to the values, attitudes and beliefs
of the Lord Jesus Christ. The first critical challenge in the practice of infant baptism is for parents, godparents and the community of faith to assume their rightful responsibilities of bringing
up children in the practice of the faith. This challenge includes
developing age-appropriate sharing of faith, life experience,
prayer, worship and scripture study. Infant baptism incorporates
children into a community of faith, which takes responsibility for
catechesis and nurturing in the faith as children grow and
develop. In the *Rite for the Baptism of Children* it is clear that parents and godparents speak on behalf of the children. The challenge is to nurture children in the faith so that they can
eventually take their rightful place within the community of faith
and speak for themselves. The practice of infant baptism
includes only one of the three initiation sacraments—baptism.

Christian initiation is completed by confirmation and eucharist. As infants and children grow through adolescence and adulthood, they need to be catechized and nurtured to the point where the faith of their parents and godparents becomes uniquely their own.

In response to this challenge, some have suggested that the baptism of infants and children should be delayed until they can make their own commitment of faith. This strategy denies the natural instincts of parents to hand on good things to their infants and children. Others have suggested that only the infants and children of practicing Catholics should be baptized. This strategy tends to use baptism as a weapon and a punishment against parents who do not practice the faith. Still others believe that no infants or children should be baptized, but rather all should be enrolled in the catechumenate, a public ceremony indicating the desire of the parents to pass on the faith to their children, and then fully initiated through baptism, confirmation and eucharist when they reach the age of reason. This strategy places a great burden on parents and the local community of faith.[7] Infant baptism poses special challenges in dealing with the incorporation of infants and children into the community of faith. Parents who come to the church for baptism are expressing a desire to pass on the faith to their children. That desire needs to be nurtured both within the family and within the parish community.

A second challenge in the practice of infant baptism is a retrieval of Augustine's notion of original sin. Many parents bring their infants and children to the church for baptism because they want to be sure that original sin is taken away. They don't want their children to die in the state of original sin. The infant or child has not committed any deliberate act of sin. However, the infant or child is born into a world which has a history of both good and evil, and is, therefore, subject to that history of good and evil. Parents and godparents who bring their children to the church for infant baptism make promises and pledges on behalf of their children to bring them up in the faith of the church. Children need to be taught to choose good and avoid evil. We are born into a world which greatly influences our choices to sin. Hatred, violence, materialism, sexism, war, etc., are part of our history and among the choices we have available to us. Baptism orients us to choose the values of Jesus Christ, which often run contrary to the historical choices people have made. Infants and children often imitate the behavior of those around them, and most parents know the difficulty of protecting their children from evil and destructive behaviors and instilling good and healthy behaviors. The practice of infant baptism incorporates children into a family and church community dedicated to cultivating the virtues that enable believers to walk in freedom, in the light of Jesus Christ. Infant baptism presumes that both parents and church will continue the process of catechesis and nurturing in the faith so that discipleship is a real possibility and opportunity for those who are baptized. Parish communities need to accept responsibility for enabling parents to be good teachers of the faith for their children, and to enable children to be included and nurtured within the community of faith.

Summary

Through the centuries, the practice of infant baptism has been the way Christians have passed on the faith of Jesus Christ to future generations. Even though baptism requires a conversion of heart to the values of Jesus Christ and incorporation into a community of faith, the practice of infant baptism recognizes that this process of growing in discipleship is a lifelong relationship. It begins at birth and comes to completion at death. Infant baptism challenges parents, godparents and the community of faith to engage in deliberate attempts to form children in the faith so that they can eventually accept this faith as their own.

Questions for Reflection and Discussion

1. In what ways can we understand baptism as a commitment to a lifelong process of conversion? How can we extend that commitment to infants?

2. What are the commonsense foundations of a theology of original sin?

3. What factors are involved in ensuring that a baptized infant will, in fact, mature into a disciple of Jesus?

4. Why should a request for a "private" baptism be denied?

5. What are the characteristics of baptized discipleship in our time?

5

Confirmation

*K*enny hated to shine his shoes. It wasn't so much that it was hard
work. He just wasn't very good at it. No matter how much newspaper he put down he always seemed to get a dab or two of polish on the
floor. That was minimal compared to how much he got all over himself.
Shining shoes was a task he avoided at all costs.

Kenny was finishing up the family dishes, which was his chore on
Friday nights. His mother came into the kitchen and said with that tone
that told Kenny there would be no negotiation: "And when you're done
with this, I want you to shine your shoes!"

Kenny spent as much time as he could finishing up the pots and
pans. He then decided to really clean the kitchen. With about as much
energy as he did anything, he proceeded to wash down the refrigerator,
and then the stove, and then... his mother came back into the kitchen and
looked at him. That was enough. He laid down some newspaper and got
the shoe kit out of the cupboard and fetched his best shoes from his bedroom. There was no way to avoid it any longer. Besides, tomorrow Kenny
would be confirmed, and his favorite uncle was going to be his sponsor,
so taking some time to shine his shoes and think seemed to be a good idea.

Kenny reviewed the lessons he had been taught about confirmation. He wondered what the bishop would look like. He heard that the
bishop sometimes asks questions, and he was afraid that he would be
embarrassed if he didn't know the answers. He tried to remember the
seven gifts of the Holy Spirit. As he loaded up his brush with the thick
black polish, he kept counting them off on his fingers. No matter where
he started, he could only come up with six. He dabbed and counted. He
had six gifts and seven spots of polish all over his hands.

His mother came back into the kitchen and turned on the tea ket-
tle. Kenny knew he was trapped. As he had gotten older, these little chats
had become infrequent. But when he saw his mother setting up her cup

66

of tea, he knew he was in for it. He used to like these talks, but the issues facing a thirteen-year-old boy made him feel uncomfortable. His mother was just about as determined a woman as Kenny knew, and if she wanted to talk, they would talk.

"How are you feeling about tomorrow?" the mother said without any warm-up dialogue.

"Fine," said Kenny. He buffed his shoes faster than usual.

"Fine?" said his mother. She had a remarkable way of expressing disbelief and disappointment in the pronunciation of a single word.

"Well, I'm looking forward to seeing Uncle Bill. I'm a little nervous that the bishop is going to ask me questions and I won't know the answers and I'll feel like a fool. I can't remember all of the gifts of the Holy Spirit, but I guess I'm fine." That was more than Kenny thought would pop out of his mouth.

His mother sat down across the kitchen table from him as the teapot began to boil. "Kenny," she said with a warm smile and her remarkable, loving eyes, "I'm looking forward to tomorrow and I want it to be a really good day for you."

She got up and began to fix her tea. She continued talking to him over her shoulder. It seemed like she was hiding her face.

"You were very sick when you were born. Your father and I just didn't know what to do for you. Your doctors said you were very underweight. You had a lot of difficulty breathing. You developed an infection in the first couple of days of your life. We were really afraid that we were going to lose you. We took you to doctor after doctor, but one problem seemed like it led to another. We just didn't know what to do. We finally went by the church on a Sunday morning and asked the pastor to baptize you right away. He was a very nice man. He knew how scared we were. Having you baptized made us feel a lot better. We knew God would take care of you. In a few weeks you did get better. Just look at you now. You're strong and healthy and tall, and I am really proud of you."

She turned to Kenny. Kenny saw the tears in her eyes and got kind of emotional himself. "It's going to be really nice, Mom."

She sat down again with her tea. She looked him straight in the eye and said: "We didn't have any party when you were baptized. We did it so fast that Uncle Bill couldn't even be there. Tomorrow I want a big party for you. I want a party because you're alive. I want a party because I'm going to watch you make the promises we made for you at your baptism. You are standing on your own now. It's going to be a wonderful day. Even if you forget some of the gifts of the Holy Spirit, your father and I want you to know how much we love you."

With that she left the kitchen. Kenny felt awkward and good. He finished his shoes smiling and wondering how tomorrow would kind of finish up what got started when he was born.

Origins

Christian initiation includes three sacramental celebrations—baptism, confirmation and eucharist. In the case of the *Rite of Christian Initiation of Adults,* these sacramental celebrations for adults and children of catechetical age are celebrated as one at the annual Easter vigil. In the case of infants and small children, the three sacraments of initiation are celebrated over the course of many years. In many places, infants are baptized, children are eucharistized at about the age of seven, and then confirmed as teenagers. Like baptism, confirmation has its origins in the complex experience of discipleship—a lifelong relationship, a lifelong commitment to following the example and teachings of Jesus Christ. This process of Christian initiation requires a conversion of heart to the values, attitudes and beliefs of Jesus Christ, and incorporation into the community of faith.

The New Testament contains no specific mention of the sacrament of confirmation, yet the Holy Spirit is frequently mentioned as a pivotal sign of the kingdom of God and as the origin of the sacrament. The *Catechism of the Catholic Church* reminds us that the Old Testament prophets taught that the spirit of the Lord would be present in the promised messiah. This prophetic teaching was confirmed when the Holy Spirit descended on Jesus during his baptism by John. But the Holy Spirit of God descends on all those who participate in the mission of Jesus through discipleship and baptism into the kingdom of God. Through the preaching of the apostles, and especially the pentecost experience, all of the baptized received the gift of the Holy Spirit. The letter to the Hebrews explicitly states that through the instruction of the apostles and the laying on of hands, the gift of the spirit is given to the baptized. This imposition of hands is recognized in the Catholic tradition as the origin of the sacrament of confirmation.[1]

Confirmation is rooted in the mission and ministry of Jesus, who is himself confirmed by God as the promised messiah at his baptism by John. Jesus promises the gift of the Holy Spirit at his resurrection and in the pentecost experience. As the disciples of Jesus Christ continued the mission and ministry of Jesus, they initiated others into the community of faith through a complex ritual which consisted of water baptism, an imposition of hands to impart the gift of the Holy Spirit, and participation in the Lord's supper. Confirmation is clearly part of the process of Christian initiation, though it is celebrated in two distinct ways. In the *Rite of Christian Initiation of Adults* it is part of a single sacramental celebration at the annual Easter vigil, but for those baptized as infants it is a separate sacramental celebration for teenagers.

Historical Developments

The New Testament gives evidence of the importance of the practice of Christian initiation, which includes water baptism, the gift of the Holy Spirit and participation in the Lord's Supper. To prepare for Christian initiation, candidates engaged in catechesis, which included preaching and proclamation of the gospel, and demonstrated that they were actively engaged in the process of conversion. Christian initiation was the culmination of this process. Baptism and confirmation were not separated. Christian initiation included the remission of sin and the imparting of the Holy Spirit.

Around the year 200, some changes occurred in the practice of Christian initiation. In the writings of Tertullian and Hippolytus we find that additions, such as an anointing with oil by the priest and another anointing with oil by the bishop, including a laying on of hands and a prayer invoking the Holy Spirit, were integral to the sacraments of initiation.[2] Perhaps the best reason for this change in Christian initiation practice is the fact that human persons quite naturally want to explain and define who they are by means of rather complex rituals. The ritual of Christian initiation was expanded in order to convey the complex

nature of the lifelong commitment of conversion to the Lord
Jesus Christ.

The *Catechism of the Catholic Church* articulates well the complexity of the ritual of Christian initiation and the various forms
it took in the eastern and western branches of Christianity.
Because of the large number of infant baptisms, the increase in
the number of parishes, and the rapid growth of dioceses, the
bishop was not able to be present at all of the baptisms. In the
west, the desire to reserve the completion of baptism to the
bishop caused the separation of confirmation from baptism. In
the east, the desire to keep the unity of Christian initiation
caused the priest to both baptize and confirm. The only involve-
ment of the bishop in Christian initiation was the fact that the
sacred chrism was blessed by the bishop. Thus, western Christian
initiation practice preserves the role of the bishop. Eastern
Christian initiation practice preserves the unity of the sacraments of baptism and confirmation.[3]

The complexity of the ritual of Christian initiation, the differences in practice between east and west, and the gradual
emergence of confirmation as a separate and unique sacrament
are due to such common factors as the increased number of people coming forward for Christian initiation after the Peace of
Constantine (313) and the inability of bishops to travel great dis-
tances to be present for Christian initiation. The east preserved
the unity of Christian initiation by continuing to celebrate all
three sacraments—baptism, confirmation and eucharist—in one
ceremony. The priest baptized, confirmed and eucharistized,
although the oil of chrism used was still consecrated by the
bishop. The west preserved the role of the bishop in Christian
initiation by separating the sacraments of Christian initiation.
The baptized waited until they could be confirmed by the
bishop, either by traveling to the cathedral or waiting until the
bishop visited their own local church. Thus, in the west, confirmation was delayed, and in many cases confirmation was never
celebrated.

The Second Vatican Council, in its *Constitution on the Sacred
Liturgy,* called for a revision of all of the church's sacramental
rites. The *Rite of Confirmation* was issued by Pope Paul VI in 1971.

It acknowledges that confirmation is practiced in two different circumstances. In the case of the Christian initiation of adults, the three sacraments of baptism, confirmation and eucharist are celebrated as one sacramental ritual at the Easter vigil. In the case of persons baptized as infants, confirmation is celebrated years later and is preceded by a period of catechesis which involves parents, a sponsor and the local parish community.[4]

Theology and Celebration of the Rite

When confirmation is celebrated as a separate sacramental rite, it is generally with persons who have been previously baptized and eucharistized as infants and children. In many places, the candidates for confirmation are teenagers. It is important to see confirmation as the completion of baptism, as the history of this sacrament clearly indicates. Confirmation is not an opportunity for teenagers to accept the Catholic faith for the first time; this theology denies the significance of infant baptism and the catechesis and nurturing in the faith which parents, godparents and the local parish community have engaged in through the years between baptism and confirmation. The rite of confirmation is an opportunity for the candidates to give evidence of their growth and development in the faith and to confirm their lived experience of discipleship and commitment to following the example and teachings of Jesus Christ.

The *Rite of Confirmation* indicates that catechesis is an essential and important preparation for the celebration of the sacrament. The candidates are instructed in the faith and associated with the Christian community in such a way that they can bear witness by living the Christian faith, especially in service to others. Teenagers who present themselves for confirmation are afforded the opportunity to reflect on their faith and to demonstrate their willingness and ability to incorporate the beliefs of the Christian community into their everyday lives. The candidates for confirmation are accompanied through this process by a sponsor, preferably one of their baptismal sponsors. The sponsor thus links baptism and confirmation, but also demonstrates that Christian initiation is a community responsibility. We come to faith within the context of Christian community, which calls us to service.[5] Local parish communities use a variety of catechetical materials and various religious experiences to nurture candidates through the process of preparing to confirm their full initiation into the Christian community.

The rite of confirmation usually takes place within the context of eucharist, celebrated by the bishop. After the liturgy of the word, the bishop gives a homily in which he explains that the candidates for confirmation, through the celebration of the sacrament, are about to take their place in the church as fully active members. In the words of the rite:

> The gift of the Holy Spirit which you are to receive will be a spiritual sign and seal to make you more like Christ and more perfect members of his Church. At his baptism by John, Christ himself was anointed by the Spirit and sent out on his public ministry to set the world on fire.

> You have already been baptized into Christ and now you will receive the power of his Spirit and the sign of the cross on your forehead. You must be witnesses before all the world to his suffering, death, and resurrection; your way of life should at all times reflect the goodness of Christ. Christ gives varied gifts to his Church, and the Spirit distributes them among the members of Christ's body to build up the holy people of God in unity and love.[6]

The bishop's role is obviously to confirm the catechesis and formation in the faith which the candidates have undergone in preparation for the celebration of this sacrament. Candidates for confirmation who were baptized as infants did not have the opportunity to engage in catechesis or to demonstrate their conversion to the Lord Jesus Christ. But their formation in the faith through the years has now prepared them to celebrate the completion of their Christian initiation and their lifelong commitment and conversion to the values, attitudes and beliefs of Jesus Christ.

After the homily, the bishop invites the candidates for confirmation to renew their baptismal promises. He then extends his hands over the candidates and prays:

All powerful God, Father of our Lord Jesus Christ, by water
and the Holy Spirit you freed your sons and daughters from
sin and gave them new life. Send your Holy Spirit upon
them to be their Helper and Guide. Give them the spirit of
wisdom and understanding, the spirit of right judgment and
courage, the spirit of knowledge and reverence. Fill them
with the spirit of wonder and awe in your presence. We ask
this through Christ our Lord. Amen.[7]

The candidates, one at a time, then come forward with their
sponsor to the bishop, who makes the sign of the cross on their
forehead with chrism, while saying "be sealed with the Gift of
the Holy Spirit."[8] The bishop then extends the sign of peace to
the newly confirmed. The liturgy of the eucharist then continues
as usual and a special blessing is given by the bishop to the newly
confirmed at the conclusion of the eucharist.

The rite clearly connects this sacrament to baptism and the
completion of the sacraments of Christian initiation. The
emphasis is on living the faith, within the context of the Christian community. The renewal of baptismal promises, the prayer
for the invocation of the Holy Spirit, and the sign of the cross
with chrism all point to the role of the Holy Spirit in the life of
Christians.

Pastoral Challenges

Christian initiation is a process of coming to faith in the
Lord Jesus Christ. Parents who baptized their infants pledged to
pass on the faith to their children through the years of their
growing to adulthood. The first challenge in the practice of confirmation is for the community of faith to take seriously its obligation to nurture everyone within the community in the faith.
Baptism is the beginning of Christian initiation; confirmation
and eucharist are further steps along the way. Parents are the
first teachers of the faith for their children. However, as children
grow and mature through the years, appropriate catechetical
materials and experiences are needed so that they can understand the faith, practice the faith, and live the values, attitudes
and beliefs of Jesus Christ. Parish communities are challenged to

take responsibility for nurturing children in the faith through catechesis and worship experiences. Parents need help in passing on the faith to their children. The separation of the three initiation sacraments often means that many never celebrate confirmation. The separation of the three initiation sacraments challenges the local parish community with the opportunity to nurture children in the faith through a process of catechesis and through gradual incorporation of children into full membership in the church.

A second challenge in the practice of confirmation is the tendency to view it as a kind of sacrament of Christian maturity. This view promotes an understanding of confirmation as an opportunity for teenagers to accept the Christian faith as their own. The problem with this view is that it tends to deny any validity to infant baptism and first eucharist. Confirmation, in this view, carries the entire burden of Christian initiation. It denies the role of parents, godparents and the local parish community in the long process of catechesis and nurturing in the faith. Confirmation is not a time for teenagers to decide whether or not they want to accept the Christian faith; as if, somehow, baptism and first eucharist were not important steps along the way. Confirmation is a ratification of baptism, as the *Rite of Confirmation* clearly indicates, not a replacement for baptism. Confirmation ratifies the process of coming to faith that began in baptism. Confirmation completes baptism in that the candidates have given evidence, through their years of growing in the faith, that the conversion begun in baptism continues in their living the Christian life. The candidates for confirmation are not celebrating the beginning of their Christian life, but rather pledging to continue their life of discipleship—a lifelong relationship, a lifelong commitment to following the example and teachings of Jesus Christ.

Summary

Confirmation is part of the process of Christian initiation, though it is celebrated in two distinct ways. In the *Rite of Christian Initiation of Adults* it is part of a single sacramental celebration at the annual Easter vigil, but for those baptized as infants it is a separate sacramental celebration for teenagers. The rite challenges the church to take seriously the fact that people come to faith through catechesis and participation in the ministry of the local parish community. For those who have been nurtured and catechized by parents, godparents and the parish community, confirmation celebrates God's gift of the Holy Spirit, first given in baptism, and now confirmed and ratified through the lived experience of the candidates.

Questions for Reflection and Discussion

1. Why is conversion at the root of the sacrament of confirmation?

2. How did confirmation get separated from baptism?

3. What is the role of the bishop in Christian initiation?

4. Why is catechesis so important for previously baptized persons who are presenting themselves for confirmation?

5. How does confirmation "ratify" the other sacraments of initiation, namely, baptism and eucharist?

6

Eucharist

*C*huck met Tina in college. They were immediately attracted to each other. They shared a common interest in the outdoors. Both had been involved in 4H clubs in their youth. Both had come from large families. Both shared similar political views and they both loved to dance. They dated for a short while and then married at midpoint in their college careers. Neither was terribly religious. Chuck had been raised a Catholic and Tina had attended a variety of Christian churches. Chuck always presumed he was a Catholic because his family was. While on his own at college it didn't seem important for him to get involved. His parents always went to church. They were taking care of the responsibility in that area. Tina didn't feel one way or the other about it.

When it came time for the wedding they decided that they would get married in the Catholic Church. There was a stronger tie there. Chuck's family had been members at Saint Cecilia's all their lives. Chuck and Tina did the necessary preparations and got the dispensations that they needed. They had a nice wedding. They did not think about it much.

Within the first year of marriage Tina became pregnant. She dropped out of school, thinking that her education was something that could be taken care of along the way. Both Chuck and Tina very much wanted the child. They knew it would be a struggle to be in school and to raise a child, but they were young and full of energy. They had a girl. Chuck stayed in school to finish. They managed. There was pressure from family to have the child baptized, and they had a nice party on the day of baptism. They didn't think much about the consequences.

Within the first five years of marriage, Chuck and Tina had three daughters. Everyone was healthy and the family was very happy. Chuck got a good job as an engineer. They bought a comfortable home. Their family life seemed to be unfolding flawlessly. The problems began when *the older two children began to attend a childcare center at the local Methodist church. The children began to ask questions about God and church and the meanings of things. Chuck and Tina decided that, since they had been blessed with three healthy children and wanted very much to raise them well, they should go back to church.*

Chuck didn't think about it much. If they were going to attend a church, they would go to Saint Cecilia's. They went. They felt very out of place. Chuck did go to confession and received communion and loved the experience. Tina just sat in the pew and tried to manage her children. She was very uncomfortable with the rituals that she did not understand. The children didn't seem to be welcome. Chuck and Tina hated arguing and so they did not. If things got difficult between them, they usually attempted to forget about it. The only problem was that the children kept asking questions and Sunday after Sunday they went to church and frequently left early because of the children.

Tina finally suggested that they try a Christian church in their neighborhood. They did. They loved it. The children were welcome. They had adult Bible study that Chuck got involved with. There was a mother's club that Tina joined. They helped her make a plan for finishing her education. They felt they had found a church for their family and all was well.

Years passed and the children began to grow. They got more and more involved with their church. Chuck began to think about his faith. He began to miss something but he wasn't sure what.

One Christmas Chuck's parents asked that the whole family get together and attend midnight mass. Tina was very comfortable about staying home with the kids and Chuck was happy to go to mass. He had good memories of his church at Christmas. It was a beautiful celebration. The decorations were great. The choirs were excellent. Chuck got quite caught up in the moment. When it came time for communion Chuck just sat down in his pew. Everyone else went up to receive. It was then that he realized what he had been missing–communion. That was it. There was something about this ritual of going up the aisle and knowing all your faults and all your needs and then receiving the body of Christ. There was something good in that. Even though he didn't receive that night, he wanted to. In fact, the want began to grow in his heart. There was something in the receiving of communion that brought it all together and made it whole. After a lot of thinking, Chuck asked

Tina how she might feel about trying to find a Catholic church where she and the children could be comfortable. She agreed only if she could become a member too. They found one. Tina was received into the church after a year. She discovered what Chuck had missed and what comfort and joy there was in just receiving communion with her family and a parish that had come to care about her.

Origins

Christians know that the eucharist has its origins in what Jesus said and did at the last supper, and in his command to "do this in memory of me." The New Testament gives us four accounts of the last supper—1 Corinthians 11:23–26, Mark 14:22–25, Matthew 26:26–29, and Luke 22:14–20. John's account of the last supper, 13:1–20, does not include Jesus' words and deeds with the bread and wine, but rather Jesus' washing the feet of his disciples. However, one of the major themes of John's gospel is Jesus as the bread of life.[1] Paul's account of the last supper is the earliest written New Testament record of this event:

> For I received from the Lord what I also handed on to you, that the Lord Jesus, on the night he was handed over, took bread, and, after he had given thanks, broke it and said, "This is my body that is for you. Do this in remembrance of me." In the same way also the cup, after supper, saying, "This cup is the new covenant in my blood. Do this, as often as you drink it, in remembrance of me." For as often as you eat this bread and drink this cup, you proclaim the death of the Lord until he comes. (1 Corinthians 11:23–26)

Within the context of the last supper Jesus followed the Jewish custom of giving praise and thanks to God with special blessing prayers over bread and wine. However, in the context of the last supper Jesus gave new meaning to these elements. In the Old Testament bread and wine were offered in sacrifice in thanksgiving to God for the harvest of the earth. In the exodus experience, commemorated in the annual celebration of Passover, Jews remembered the manna God provided for them in the desert and their dependence on God's word as the bread of their life.

At the end of the Passover meal, the final cup of wine recalls the Jewish hope in the future coming of the messiah. At the last supper, Jesus added new meaning to a familiar ritual. Jesus is the word of God and the messiah. "Jesus' passing over to his father by his death and resurrection, the new passover, is anticipated in the supper and celebrated in the eucharist, which fulfills the Jewish passover and anticipates the final passover of the church in the glory of the kingdom."[2]

While the institution of the eucharist at the last supper is usually focused on the words of Jesus over bread and wine, the context of these words within the supper in the four New Testament accounts provides a more complete understanding of the nature and meaning of eucharist. In all four New Testament accounts Jesus *took bread,* and then a cup of wine, *gave thanks* for the bread and wine, *broke* the bread and *gave* the bread and the cup to the disciples. Eucharist is thus an activity of the church—taking, giving thanks, breaking and giving. Jesus' words of blessing are intimately connected with his deeds.

The account of the words and deeds of Jesus at the last supper, so carefully preserved in all four New Testament accounts, suggests that eucharist, flowing from the last supper, was a familiar ritual of prayer and thanksgiving for the followers of Jesus. An examination of the miracle of the multiplication of the loaves enhances the understanding of the ritualized nature of the eucharist. This miracle story is reported six times in the four gospels—Mark 6:34–44 and 8:1–10, Matthew 14:13–21 and 15:32–39, Luke 9:10–17 and John 6:1–15. In all six accounts the same activity is present. Jesus takes bread, gives thanks for the bread, breaks the bread and gives it to the disciples to distribute to the people. The four New Testament accounts of the last supper, the six stories of the multiplication of the loaves, and the many occasions when Jesus shared a meal with people, especially with sinners and the postresurrection meals with his disciples, all point to the fact that the eucharist has its origins in the ministry, passion, death and resurrection of Jesus Christ. The *Catechism of the Catholic Church* teaches us that the eucharist is the memorial of Christ's passover. When Jews celebrate Passover they not only remember the past historical event of God liberating them from slavery in Egypt, they also experience in the present moment the liberating grace of God in the reality of the here and now. When Christians celebrate eucharist they not only remember the past historical event of the ministry, passion, death and resurrection of Jesus Christ, they also experience in the present moment the passover of Christ and the reality of the liberating grace of God in the reality of the here and now.[3]

When the church gathers to celebrate eucharist it does not merely re-enact what Jesus said and did at the last supper, just as when Jews celebrate Passover they do not merely re-enact that historical event. The eucharist is a memorial—the remembrance of a past historical event of great significance, because that event is still significant today, and because that event must always be significant in the future. This unique style of remembering, *anamnesis,* makes Christ present and recalls the great works of God, through Jesus Christ, which are always present in the Christian community when it celebrates the eucharist.

The eucharist has its origins in the ministry of Jesus, who was formed and influenced by the prayer and worship of Israel. However, the New Testament accounts of the last supper clearly signify a new meaning and a new direction for the followers of Jesus Christ.

Historical Developments

After the death and resurrection of Jesus, the disciples gathered to celebrate the eucharist on a regular basis, but they continued to worship in the synagogues on the Sabbath. The Sabbath synagogue service consisted of readings from the Torah and the Prophets, instruction from the rabbis, and prayers and blessings from the Psalms. The eucharist was celebrated in family homes on Saturday evening and Sunday morning within the context of a fellowship meal. The fellowship meal quickly disappeared from the celebration of the eucharist, but participation in worship in the Jerusalem temple and the local synagogues continued for several decades. It was probably not until the destruction of the Jerusalem temple in 70 C.E. that the followers of Jesus Christ clearly understood themselves as a distinct and new religious tradition.

The first Christian document, outside of the New Testament, to mention the eucharist is the *Didache,* a word which means teachings, written at the end of the first or beginning of the second century. Chapter fourteen contains the following description of the eucharist:

> On the dominical day of the Lord, come together to break bread and give thanks, after having, in addition, confessed your sins so that your sacrifice may be pure. But let anyone who is at odds with his fellow not join with you until he has first been reconciled, lest your sacrifice be profaned. For here is what the Lord says: "In every place and at all times let them offer me a pure sacrifice, for I am a great king, says the Lord, and my name is wonderful among the nations."[4]

Several important elements of the eucharist are in place at this early date. Christians gather on Sunday, the first day of the week, and not on Saturday, the last day of the week. Sunday was chosen because it was the day God inaugurated creation and the day God raised Jesus from the dead. The eucharist is a prayer of thanksgiving within the context of the assembly of Christians, and is clearly the activity of taking, blessing, breaking and giving bread and wine in memory of Jesus Christ. The current practice of the penitential prayers prior to the actual memorial of the last supper is an early historical development and testifies to the reconciling nature of eucharist. At approximately the same time, Ignatius of Antioch indicates: "The only eucharist to be considered legitimate is the one celebrated under the presidency of the bishop or of someone he has appointed."[5]

Justin the Martyr provides a more complete description of the eucharist in a document known as the *First Apology,* written several decades after the *Didache.* In chapter sixty-seven Justin provides the following description of the eucharist:

> On the day named after the sun, all who live in city or countryside assemble in the same place. The memoirs of the apostles or the writings of the prophets are read for as long as time allows. When the lector has finished, the president

addresses us and exhorts us to imitate the splendid things
we have heard. Then we all stand and pray. As we said earlier, when we have finished praying, bread, wine, and water
are brought up. The president then prays and gives thanks
according to his ability. And the people give their assent
with an "Amen!" Next, the gifts, which have been "eucharis-
tified" are distributed, and everyone shares in them, while
they are also sent via the deacons to the absent brethren.[6]

Justin's description of the eucharist indicates that there is a Sunday assembly for eucharist that includes a liturgy of the word,
with readings from the Old Testament and the New Testament,
followed by a homily and prayers of the faithful and a liturgy of
the eucharist, with the bringing forward of bread and wine, a
eucharistic or thanksgiving prayer and communion for those
present and those absent. The assembly is organized under the
leadership of a president who presides at the activity of
eucharist, which obviously needs the active participation of the
assembly to celebrate the memorial of the words and deeds of
Jesus Christ at the last supper.

During the first three centuries, until the peace of Constantine in 313 C.E., Christians were persecuted for their faith in
Jesus Christ. One practical effect of this persecution is the lim-
ited amount of historical evidence on how Christians celebrated
the eucharist. In order to protect themselves, Christians kept
quiet. Christians prepared candidates for initiation very carefully
and quietly. This preparation period, called the catechumenate,
may have lasted for several years, and candidates were not permitted to be present for the liturgy of the eucharist until their initiation, which included baptism, confirmation and eucharist.
The full meaning of Christian initiation was not explained to the
candidates until after their full initiation into the church.
Eucharist, the culmination of the initiation sacraments, completed initiation. Once fully initiated, Christians celebrated
eucharist on a weekly basis.

With the peace of Constantine, Christianity became a legitimate world religion, and the religion of the Roman empire. As a
legitimate world religion, Christianity began the long process of
accommodating large numbers of people into the community of

faith. In the beginning Christians met for worship in private homes, but with the peace of Constantine, larger meeting halls, and eventually church buildings became the norm. As Christianity spread throughout the world a gradual process of standardization occurred in the celebration of the eucharist. The original, somewhat informal gatherings for the celebration of the eucharist became highly structured and formal gatherings, which included standardized rituals and prayers. Latin became the official and universal language of the eucharist, which was presided over by a bishop or priest who read the official prayers and did all that was necessary for the celebration. The people watched the bishop or priest celebrate the eucharist. The ancient custom of reserving the eucharist for the sick and dying gradually led to the practice of placing tabernacles in churches, often on the altar, and the custom of eucharistic devotion tended to overshadow the actual celebration of the eucharist.[7] The Catholic tradition of worship of the eucharist at mass and outside of mass is summarized in the *Catechism of the Catholic Church*. In the eucharist, Christians express their faith in the real presence of Christ under the appearance of bread and wine. Christians show reverence for this presence by genuflecting or bowing and by cultivating a spirit of adoration for the eucharist both during mass and outside of it. The tabernacle first emerged within Christianity as a place for reserving the eucharist so that it could be brought to the sick and those unable to participate in mass. But the tabernacle soon became a popular focus for prayer and adoration, and a visible sign of the real presence of Christ.[8]

During the Middle Ages, as the church was trying to respond to the needs of a large, universal population of Christians and several major controversies and heresies, the theology of Thomas Aquinas and the teachings of the Council of Trent greatly influenced eucharistic theology and understanding until the Second Vatican Council. Aquinas masterfully combined the classical understanding of eucharist as symbol with the philosophical understanding of Aristotle. Aquinas believed that the bread and wine of the eucharist was substantially changed into the real presence of Christ, though the accidents of bread and wine remained. Transubstantiation became the Catholic word to explain this transformation. Aquinas' theology helped the church negotiate a difficult historical period, yet he himself still believed that the eucharist was a mystery which no amount of philosophy or theology could ever hope to master.[9]

The Catholic response to the Protestant Reformation, the Council of Trent, basically sanctioned the theology of Thomas Aquinas, which prevailed in the church until the Second Vatican Council. By the close of the Middle Ages Christians had lost sight of the eucharist as a community meal. Eucharist was not so much an action of the assembled community as community witness to the presence of Christ in the bread and wine. The reception of communion was infrequent, and when people did receive communion it was in the mouth, lest their dirty hands touch the sacred bread.

The contemporary renewal of eucharistic theology and practice began in the late nineteenth and early twentieth centuries. Biblical and liturgical scholars throughout the world began to study the origins of the eucharist and to suggest strategies for renewal. In the early years of the twentieth century, Pope Pius X encouraged more frequent reception of the eucharist and set the age for first communion at the age of discretion, approximately the age of seven. In the middle of the twentieth century, Pope Pius XII introduced some liturgical reforms dealing with the eucharist. All of this prepared the way for the *Constitution on the Sacred Liturgy,* issued by the Second Vatican Council in 1963. The reforms set in motion by Vatican II affected all of the sacramental rituals of the church, but the most noticeable were the reforms in the celebration of the eucharist. These included the use of vernacular languages, the practice of the reception of communion in the hand and under the species of both bread and wine, an enhanced liturgy of the word, the publication of many eucharistic prayers, the turning of the altar so that the presider faced the people, the development of various lay ministers to assist in the celebration of the eucharist, congregational singing, and an expanded theology of Christ present in the assembly, the word, the bread and wine, and the presider. Dennis C. Smolarski, S.J., summarizes the renewal of the eucharist, begun at Vatican II, in this way:

If our reading of the Acts of the Apostles and early Christian writings is correct, from the earliest days Christians gathered to celebrate the eucharist. Thus, in one sense, to be the Church is to celebrate the eucharist....

The eucharist is the family banquet of all who constitute the Church. It is the meal at which all are fed, at which no one is a foreigner. Rich and poor, powerful and powerless, old and young, landowners and the homeless are all welcome at the one table at which Christ once again feeds his people.

The intimate interconnection between Church and eucharist is a dynamic, active relationship. The differences between the old missal and the new all point to the reality that the eucharist is not primarily the static elements reserved in the tabernacle but rather the active celebration of giving thanks in memory of the death and resurrection of Jesus. This dynamic celebration of memory-filled thanksgiving by the assembly of Christians is the core of what "eucharist" is about. It is in gathering for eucharist that individual Christians become the Church.[10]

For Christians more familiar with the pre-Vatican II celebration of the eucharist, the reforms of Vatican II seem new and different. However, the reformed celebration of the eucharist is actually a retrieval of more ancient and wholistic notions of eucharistic theology and practice which focus on the activity of taking bread and wine, giving thanks for them, breaking them and giving them to the community in memory of the ministry, passion, death and resurrection of the Lord Jesus Christ, present and active in the community of faith.

Theology and Celebration of the Rite

Adults who are initiated into the church at the Easter vigil experience the eucharist as the culmination of initiation. They are baptized, confirmed and invited to the eucharistic table for the first time. During their time of preparation for initiation they participated in the liturgy of the word with the assembly, but were dismissed from the assembly at the conclusion of the liturgy of the word. Only after baptism and confirmation were they invited to participate in the liturgy of the eucharist. Baptized infants begin their preparation for the eucharist at the age of discretion, approximately age seven, which culminates in their celebration of "first communion." These children usually celebrate confirmation as teenagers. In both cases, Sunday eucharist becomes the regular pattern of their Christian life within the community of faith. To be a Christian means to participate Sunday after Sunday with a community that celebrates the eucharist. The eucharist makes the church.

The best way to understand the theology of the eucharist is to participate in the eucharist. And the best document which articulates the theology of the eucharist is the "General Instruction of the Roman Missal" (GIRM).[11] The reforms set in motion by the Second Vatican Council in the celebration of the eucharist are richly detailed in this document.

The GIRM indicates that "all in the assembly gathered for mass have an individual right and duty to contribute their participation in ways differing according to the diversity of their order and liturgical function."[12] Eucharist begins with the assembly, the people, gathered in the name of Jesus Christ. While the details of the environment in which people gather, the occasion on which people gather, and the manner in which people gather are not unimportant, eucharist is about people. People gather with a purpose at eucharist. As people assemble, they recognize that it is the Lord Jesus Christ who has called them together in his name. The assembly needs a presider, a priest or bishop, who gathers the assembly together and enables them to remember who they are and why they have gathered. "He therefore presides over the assembly and leads its prayer, proclaims the message of salvation, joins the people to himself in offering the sacrifice to the Father through Christ in the Spirit, gives them the bread of eternal life, and shares it with them."[13]

The assembly gathered for eucharist needs a presider, a priest or bishop, but also many others who participate in various ministries which are designed to enable the assembly to give praise and thanks to God. The presence of these ministers witnesses to the fact that eucharist is celebrated by the assembly. Among the ministers needed for eucharist are the following: a deacon, acolytes, lectors, cantors, musicians, special ministers of the eucharist, ushers or hospitality ministers, liturgical planners. The post-Vatican II celebration of the eucharist clearly emphasizes the general role of the assembly and the many specific ministries required for eucharistic celebration. Obviously, planning, training and coordination are key elements which involve the participation of the assembly in the eucharist.

The structure of the eucharist articulates its theology. The basic structure for every eucharist includes the following: introductory rites, liturgy of the word, preparation of the gifts, liturgy of the eucharist, and concluding rites.

The purpose of the introductory rites is to gather the assembly into one place, as one body, to give praise and thanks to God, in the name of Jesus Christ. This is accomplished through a procession of both assembly and ministers to their places within the church. Music and singing help focus the assembly on their unity in the Lord Jesus Christ. The presider moves to the presidential chair to lead the assembly in the sign of the cross, the greeting, the penitential prayers, the gloria, and the opening prayer. These rites are introductory in that they unite the assembly in focusing their attention on God and on the purpose of their gathering.

Eucharist quickly proceeds to attending to the word of God, peacefully, slowly and deliberately. The liturgy of the word usually consists of a reading from the Old Testament, a sung psalm response, a reading from one of the New Testament letters, the alleluia or other chant, the gospel, the homily, the profession of faith, and the general intercessions. The liturgy of the word, as revised by the Second Vatican Council, provides for an increased use of scripture in the life of the church. There is a three-year cycle of readings for Sundays and solemnities and a two-year cycle for weekdays. God's word stands at the center of the life of the Christian community because only God's word gives life. In the GIRM, the purpose of this expanded use of scripture is explained:

> In the readings, the table of God's word is laid before the
> people and the treasures of the Bible are opened to them.
> When the sacred scriptures are read in church, God himself
> is speaking to his people, and Christ, present in his word, is
> proclaimed in his Gospel. Hence the readings from God's
> word are among the most important elements in the liturgy,
> and all who are present should listen to them with rever-
> ence. The word of God in the scripture readings is indeed
> addressed to all men of all times and can be understood by
> them; yet its power to influence men is increased if it be
> given a living explanation by means of a homily which
> should be ranked as an integral part of the liturgical action.[14]

The assembly takes to heart the word of God as proclaimed in
the three-year cycle of the lectionary and, by means of the
homily, is led to a living explanation of the word, present and
active in the assembly of believers. The profession of faith presents the assembly with the opportunity to renew their baptismal
promises, in light of the word of God; the general intercessions
present the assembly with the opportunity to intercede with God
to continue God's saving activity through the lives of the assembly of the baptized.

The preparation of the gifts is a kind of transitional rite
from the liturgy of the word to the liturgy of the eucharist. The
essential purpose of this transition rite is the preparation of the
altar for the celebration of the liturgy of the eucharist. Representatives of the assembly join in a procession, usually accompanied
by music and singing, to bring forward bread and wine and others gifts to meet the needs of the church and the poor.[15] A table-
cloth is placed on the altar, along with the gifts of bread and
wine. The word of God is never enough. Action makes the word
come alive. The word evokes a response—gifts of simple bread
and wine. The assembly presents bread and wine which will eventually be brought back to the assembly for nourishment and
refreshment. The assembly gathers for a purpose—they are hungry, thirsty people. Nothing will satisfy the assembly's hunger or
quench its thirst but this bread and wine. The bread of life and
the cup of eternal salvation enable the assembly to proclaim the
word, to live the word, to be the word. The world is hungry, and

this assembly intends to feed not just itself, but the entire world. As the assembly brings forth the bread and wine, the representatives of the assembly enable all gathered to begin to understand what it means to do what Jesus did, to follow in the footsteps of him who is the bread of life and the cup of eternal salvation.

The liturgy of the eucharist begins with the introductory dialogue between the presider and the assembly, and proceeds to the preface, the eucharistic prayer, the Lord's Prayer, the sign of peace, the breaking of the bread and pouring of the wine, and the communion. There are over eighty different prefaces, depending on the liturgical season or feast, and ten eucharistic prayers. Under the leadership of its presider, the assembly, which has just *taken* bread and wine, now *gives thanks* for bread and wine, *breaks* the bread and *gives* the bread and wine back to the assembly. This activity of eucharist is accomplished during the liturgy of the eucharist.

The center of the liturgy of the eucharist is the great prayer of thanksgiving, the eucharistic prayer. The *Catechism of the Catholic Church* describes the five components of this prayer. The first is the *preface,* which begins with the introductory dialogue between presider and assembly. In the preface we give thanks to God, "through Christ, in the Holy Spirit, for all his works: creation, redemption, and sanctification." The second component is the *epiclesis,* which asks God to send the Holy Spirit upon the gifts of bread and wine so that they may become the body and blood of Christ, and so that the assembly may be united in one body and spirit. The third component is the *institution narrative,* which enables the assembly to remember that through "the power of the words and action of Christ, and the power of the Holy Spirit," Christ is sacramentally present in the bread and wine. The fourth component is the *anamnesis,* in which the assembly remembers the passion, resurrection and glorification of Christ. The fifth component is the *intercessions,* which binds the assembly to the universal church. In the intercessions the assembly prays for the church, the pope, the bishops and clergy, the living and the dead. All of the church's eucharistic prayers contain these five components.[16]

In the eucharistic prayer, the presider prays on behalf of the assembly and with the enthusiastic response of the assembly.

The assembly thanks the God who created and creates, who called Jesus of Nazareth to speak his word definitively, who gifts the assembly with the Holy Spirit. The assembly prays in thanksgiving for the eucharist it now celebrates, for the prophets and the kings, for the saints and the sinners, for the living and the dead, for the church throughout the world, for the presence and action of God's Spirit. The assembly prays in thanksgiving for all that was, all that is and all that will be. The assembly is thankful, more than words can ever express. The presider enables the assembly to voice its heartfelt thanks; to move one step closer to real communion with the Lord of life.

The conclusion to the liturgy of the eucharist is communion. The assembly prays together the Lord's Prayer and shares the peace of Jesus Christ. After the bread has been broken and the wine poured, the assembly walks forward in procession, usually accompanied by music and singing, to be nourished by the bread of life and refreshed by the cup of eternal salvation. The gifts the assembly gave have come back to them—"Give and gifts will be given to you; a good measure, packed together, shaken down, and overflowing, will be poured into your lap" (Luke 6:38). The assembly is now connected in a solemn bond of unity, peace, trust and faith. The assembly is nourished and refreshed. This is a sacred moment. Words and gestures fail to express the richness of the meaning of this moment. The ministers of the eucharist enable the assembly to commune with one another and with the God who is present.

The concluding rites mark the transition between the liturgy of word and eucharist to the work of being Christian in the world. The rite itself is very simple. There is a concluding prayer, some brief announcements, a blessing and the dismissal of the assembly, usually followed by a procession, with music and singing, of the ministers and the assembly. The final words of the presider, "Go in peace to love and serve the Lord," articulate the continued work of eucharist in the life of the Christian community in the home, the neighborhood, the workplace and the world. The assembly has gathered, the word has been proclaimed, the bread has been broken and shared. But the work is not done. The assembly, which gathered for a purpose, now

departs with a purpose. There will be tensions and disappoint-
ments in the world, but these are inevitable. The assembly has
been nourished and refreshed in the eucharist. They are now
more aware of who they are and what God calls them to be. The
assembly is bread for the world. Their lives will be broken, but
that is to be expected. They can be nourished and refreshed
again and again and again. The presider enables the assembly to
have courage and to build bridges. The assembly is a "pilgrim
people" so they must travel. Along the way they will celebrate
many other eucharists to sustain their loving and their serving in
the name of the Lord Jesus Christ. In the words of the Second
Vatican Council:

> For it is the liturgy through which, especially in the divine
> sacrifice of the Eucharist, "the work of our redemption is
> accomplished," and it is through the liturgy, especially, that
> the faithful are enabled to express in their lives and manifest
> to others the mystery of Christ and the real nature of the true
> Church.... The liturgy daily builds up those who are in the
> Church, making of them a holy temple of the Lord, a
> dwelling-place for God in the Spirit, to the mature measure
> of the fullness of Christ. At the same time it marvelously
> increases their power to preach Christ and thus show forth
> the Church, a sign lifted up among the nations, to those who
> are outside, a sign under which the scattered children of God
> may be gathered until there is one fold and one shepherd.[17]

The eucharist reminds the assembly that they are created to
make spaces for others, to make the world more hospitable, to
welcome the stranger and all others in need of a place of secu-
rity, and a future. In the eucharist the assembly experiences wisdom that saves, hope that frees, weaknesses that strengthen. In
the eucharist loneliness is assuaged and friendship is fashioned.
In the eucharist the assembly celebrates and gives thanks that
God is hidden and dwelling in forests and earth, among the poor
and the outcast, the children and the old, the mothers and the
fathers, and in whoever believes in God's love and desire to stay
with us.[18] In the eucharistic assembly, more than anywhere else,
God forms us into a holy temple, a dwelling-place for God's
spirit. Here, more than anywhere else, the fullness of Christ is

revealed in us so that we can preach the Christ who gathers all people into a communion of love and service. The eucharist enables the assembly to be the body of Christ.

Pastoral Challenges

The eucharist makes the church. The first challenge in celebrating eucharist is to continually renew our understanding of the fact that eucharist is what distinguishes Catholic Christians and makes us who we are as followers of the Lord Jesus Christ. Christians do not "attend" eucharist but rather "celebrate" eucharist. Eucharist is an activity of the church—an activity of taking, giving thanks, breaking and giving. Christians take the word of God, give thanks for the word of God, break open the word of God to explore its meaning, and give the word of God a living expression, because, as believers they incorporate the mystery and insight of the word into their daily lives. Christians take bread and wine, give God thanks for bread and wine, break and share the bread and wine, and give to one another the bread of life and the cup of eternal salvation. This activity extends far beyond Sunday eucharist. Nourished at the table of word and the table of eucharist, Christians take their very lives, give God thanks for their lives, break open their lives and give their lives in service of the kingdom of God throughout the world. Eucharist is the activity of those fully initiated into the Christian community. It is the activity of giving our lives, in memory of Jesus Christ, for the redemption and salvation of the world.

A second challenge in celebrating eucharist is the notion of a gathered community seeking nourishment through word and eucharist, and a dispersed community seeking love and service of the Lord through corporate ethical commitments and ministry. The very nature of liturgical assembly provides

> ...a vision of what we might strive for in other areas of ecclesial life. Participation in the assembly can also be an experience of "ritual play" for the community. It is an opportunity for the community to reconfigure its relationships and responsibilities and arrive at new insight into its self-understanding and its way of being in the world. In fact, such "ritual

play" is already going on and we need to draw wisdom from the experience.[19]

Through the transforming power of the eucharist we recognize our corporate mission of telling the story of God's self-disclosure and self-giving in the gracious moments of our own lives, and our partnership with the community of faith. We come to life through our participation in community—a partnership which helps us form a sense of sin, responsibility, membership, memory and imagination. Through the transforming power of the eucharistic assembly we respond to God's call for our service, mission and vocation in the world. Here, in eucharistic assembly, we devote ourselves to a life in common, for the common good.[20]

A third challenge in celebrating eucharist is to take to heart the transformative power of the one table, the one loaf and the one cup, which challenges us to be an inclusive community. God's invitation to communion at the table challenges our discrimination and disunity in all areas of our lives. Theological reflection upon gathering at the eucharistic table must begin with thoughts of the countless victims which discrimination has created. And the quality of our theological reflection at the eucharistic table will be judged by its power to create a future of equality, diversity and mutuality in which God's commonwealth of justice and peace will prevail.

A fourth challenge in celebrating eucharist is the continuing discussion of the issue of Sunday celebrations in the absence of a priest.[21] The discussion is painful and slow, and in the process we may experience for a time the dissolution of eucharist as the central act of our church. Because of the growing shortage of priests, many Catholic communities are not able to celebrate Sunday eucharist on a regular basis. Sunday celebrations in the absence of a priest are not eucharist. These worship services usually include a liturgy of the word, followed by a communion service. The provision for these services does enable a parish community to gather on Sunday for worship, but not for eucharist. This is a serious departure from Catholic tradition. The challenge for the future is to be faithful to our Catholic tradition of Sunday eucharist and to deal forthrightly and courageously with our responsibility to be a eucharistic community.

A fifth challenge in celebrating eucharist is the "... full, conscious, and active participation in liturgical celebrations."[22] Celebrating eucharist requires a diversity of ministries, and, most important of all, an assembly. Selection, training, coordination and ongoing formation for all involved in eucharistic celebration is an obvious need and challenge. In addition to all within the eucharistic assembly understanding their purpose, roles and duties, they need to understand that eucharist is celebrated during the various cycles and seasons of the liturgical year. The eucharist is never celebrated in isolation. Sunday eucharist is celebrated on particular days, within particular seasons of the church year, during particular times in the life of the worshipping community, praying with assigned scriptures and prayers, all designed to enable the assembly to hear the word of God, not as ancient historical text but as the living word of God spoken to us this day, in our time and history. Each of the seasons of the church year—the Paschal Triduum, Lent, Easter, Advent, Christmas, and Ordinary Time—present special challenges because of the time of year, the liturgical season, the assigned scriptures and prayers, and the special circumstances of the world in which we live.

Summary

The eucharist makes the church. It is the completion of Christian initiation. To be Christian means to participate Sunday after Sunday with a community that celebrates the eucharist. Participation in the eucharist is a celebration of our lifelong initiation into the mystery of Christ and his church. In the eucharist, Christians give God thanks for all that they are, for all that they have, and for all that exists. The eucharist is the mystery of what we are and what we receive. It is the mystery of Christ in us.

Questions for Reflection and Discussion

1. How does the miracle story of the multiplication of the loaves and fishes help us to understand what eucharist is all about?

2. There are five elements of the basic structure of the eucharist: intro-ductory rites, liturgy of the word, preparation of the gifts, liturgy of the eucharist, and concluding rites. How do these elements flow one to the other? How do they help us keep a memorial of what Jesus did?

3. Discuss the effects of eucharist on the community. How is the com-munity nurtured? What is the community challenged to do?

4. How does eucharist "make" the church?

THE SACRAMENTS OF HEALING

✝ ✝ ✝

7

Reconciliation

*M*ark was O.K. He would not describe himself as happy or unhappy. He was just O.K.

He enjoyed his fortieth birthday. His wife of eighteen years had thrown him a small party where he had received the usual fortyish kind of gifts, those that were supposed to remind him that he was rapidly growing old. There were silly things. Ann had asked her guests to bring only gag gifts and they did. Most of the gifts, like the belly burner and the vitamin tablets, came wrapped in black paper. There was a lot of laughter and a lot of comment about the effects of Father Time. Mark, however, was O.K. about it all.

It was probably because of the birthday that Mark began to think a lot about his life. He was a good husband. He liked being a father. He did his job well. No complaints. But there was no joy either.

Mark and Ann married young. They were both in college. It was a struggle to make ends meet. They managed. They became pregnant in the first year of marriage. They had a son, Mark Jr., who was a real joy to them, particularly in those early years when they had to use all of their wits just to get by. Mark and Ann spent a lot of time around his birthday reminiscing about the fun of those early years. They remembered how they used to laugh while counting out pennies just to eat before payday. It was a scary time, but it was also a fun time.

Mark worked as a bookkeeper for the same small company all of his working life. There was always enough work to do. Things got better for them as their marriage unfolded. He earned more. Ann began a teaching career which she loved. With their two incomes, they were really quite comfortable. They congratulated themselves frequently about not falling apart during the lean years. Mark Jr. was a clumsy sort of kid. He was not particularly good at anything but was involved in everything. As Mark Jr. was finishing high school, it seemed that he was always out doing something. They had begun to talk about the need to schedule some family times together. But everything was O.K.

Mark and Ann married in the Catholic Church. They had their son baptized. They got involved in little ways, particularly around his first communion. It was hard to say what happened. There was no fight with the church. Most of the priests they met were good. They liked the people in the community well enough. Little by little they had just drifted away. They called themselves Catholics, but they had even given up the basics of Christmas and Easter.

It began to bother Mark as he began his fortieth year. Whatever happened to all of that stuff? He didn't know who the pastor was, even though the parish church was just down the block from their house. They didn't know any people who went to that church anymore. They had few friends anyway, and the friends they had didn't seem to be interested either. Mark began to realize that something was missing in his life, something that had to do with being connected, being involved. It surprised him to realize how much he had been thinking about going back to church.

He didn't want to bother Ann about it. Mark Jr. didn't seem to need it. It was going to have to be Mark's deal and Mark's deal alone. He just didn't know where to start.

After a few weeks of mulling it over, Mark decided he should give church a try one more time. However, a huge sinking feeling came over him. If he went back to church he would have to go to confession. He had never particularly liked that part of Catholic life. He remembered how embarrassing it was to admit to some priest that you didn't even know that you were not perfect. He wondered how he would ever count up all of the missed masses, how many years of no Easter duty, how many lies, how many.... Wow!

He remembered some things about an examination of conscience. He even remembered the act of contrition. In fact, while he had let most of his religious practices slide, saying an act of contrition from time to time seemed to make him feel good. But he couldn't remember the difference between a mortal sin and a venial sin. He knew he wasn't a bad person. He had just become an uninteresting person. He wondered if that was grounds for mortal sin.

He read the sign at the corner of the church that confessions were heard at 4:00 every Saturday afternoon. Mark didn't say anything to

*anybody. He just went in. He was amazed when he walked into the
church. There was an unmistakable smell to a Catholic Church. What
was that smell? Old incense or beeswax? Maybe it was just the smell of
an old, well-used building. There was something quite comfortable
about just being there. The place looked good, well-kept and freshly
painted. The only problem was that he could not find the confessional.
There was a statue in a niche that used to be where the box was. Mark
was a little confused.*

*He was happy that there was no one around. He sat in a back pew
and enjoyed the quiet. He began to think deeply about what he would
say when he went to confession, if he could find out where the confessional was. He really didn't do anything that was terribly wrong. He
thought that the priest would find him really boring. But as he thought
about himself he began to become aware of the fact that the only thing he
really felt guilty about was that, of the many things he had let go, he had
let go of his relationship with his father. He wondered long and hard
about how that had happened. When Mark Jr. was young they seemed
to do all kinds of things together. Lately it seemed that they couldn't get
their dates together. There was no fight or any disappointment. They
had just grown apart.*

*A few older women came into the church. They smiled at Mark
and then walked down to the front of the church where the priest's sacristy used to be. They formed an unmistakable line. Ah, that's where
they moved it. Mark watched them intensely and tried to figure out
what he was going to say. Some others came. It was wonderfully quiet
there and peaceful. He decided he would just go in there and blurt out,
"I don't know how to start. I have been away for a long time."*

*After a while there was no line. Mark took a deep breath and went
down the aisle to what he figured would be the confessional box. Just as
he arrived at the door a young priest walked out. He startled Mark, who
blurted out, "Sorry, I used to go here, I was just looking around." The
young priest shook his hand and welcomed him. "Come in and see our
new reconciliation room. We are really proud of it."*

*Mark looked in to see a bright, pleasant room with a crucifix.
There was a kneeler and a screen, but there were also two chairs sitting
face to face. The priest explained that a person could make a confession
anonymously behind the screen, or could sit down and talk to the priest
face to face.*

Mark was sure he was not ready for that. He thanked the priest and walked out of the church as fast as he could, but on the way home he became disappointed with himself. He should have given it a try. Too late now. But he continued to think about getting some life back. He promised himself he would go next week. Maybe he would even talk to Ann. Perhaps they could go together. He was sure he would go and things would get better.

Mark came into the house and met Ann. He told her that he had just been out for a long walk. Then he said, "I think I am going to call my dad."

Origins

The sacrament of reconciliation has its origins in the ministry of Jesus. The synoptic gospels present Jesus as the one sent from God to proclaim the message of the kingdom and to urge people to repent and believe in the gospel.[1] The *Catechism of the Catholic Church* links the origin of reconciliation to Jesus' first appearance to the disciples after the resurrection. Jesus greets the disciples with his gift of peace, and then confers on them the power to forgive sins.[2] While Jesus believed that only God forgives sins, he claimed the authority to forgive sins in the name of God.[3] Since Christ entrusted to the disciples the ministry of reconciliation, all those ordained through the sacrament of holy orders have the power to forgive sins in the name of God.[4]

In a broader context, the sacrament of reconciliation has its origins in the ministry, passion, death and resurrection of Jesus Christ. As the gospels teach us, Jesus began his public ministry by participating in the baptism of John—a baptism of repentance for the forgiveness of sins. Jesus urged repentance, a turning away from sin in all its dimensions, and conversion, a turning to God and a life of loving service to one's neighbor. Much of the ministry and teaching of Jesus focused on reconciling sinners to God and the community. Jesus forgave the sins of the paralytic and restored him to bodily health (Mk 2:1–12); Jesus taught us to pray for the forgiveness of our sins (Lk 11:4 and Mt 6:12); Jesus taught the disciples the importance of giving good example to others (Mk 9:42–48); Jesus taught the disciples the importance of forgiving those who sin against us and the dire consequences for those who do not forgive (Lk 18:15–35); and in the powerful parable of the prodigal son (Lk 15:11–32) Jesus demonstrated the unbounded and unconditional love and mercy of God toward those who acknowledge their sinfulness and engage in a life of conversion and repentance. Jesus' ministry and teaching clearly demonstrate the central place of reconciliation in the Christian life. Jesus healed and forgave, and entrusted to his church the task of being a healing and forgiving community.

The sacrament of reconciliation has its origins, therefore, in the human experience of sin and alienation. Estrangement and alienation are part of human experience. Throughout the entire course of our lives we yearn to be made whole, to be restored, renewed and reconciled. Throughout the entire course of our lives we struggle to name the evil and sin in ourselves, in others, and in the social and institutional structures which frame our world. Sin is both personal and communal, but there is really no such thing as a private sin. All sin has social and communal consequences. Each person's goodness contributes to the building up of the community; each person's sin contributes to the tearing down of the community. Sin offends God, and ruptures our relationship with God, and offends the church, and ruptures our relationship with the community of faith. In the sacrament of reconciliation we seek to restore our relationship with both God and the church.[5]

Historical Developments

The church has always had a variety of ways to forgive sins. The Acts of the Apostles tells us that on the day of Pentecost, Peter told the people that they should be baptized for the forgiveness of sins.[6] The church has always believed that it had the power to forgive sins through Jesus' spirit and has provided a variety of ways and several sacraments for the forgiveness of sins. The *Catechism of the Catholic Church* lists the following forms of penance for Christians: fasting (conversion to oneself), prayer (conversion to God), and almsgiving (conversion to others); daily gestures of reconciliation, care for the poor, defending justice, personal admission of faults to others, spiritual direction, reading scripture, eucharist and reconciliation.[7]

The first sacrament of reconciliation is baptism. As we have described in the chapters on the *Rite of Christian Initiation of Adults* and infant baptism, baptism is the first and premier sacrament of reconciliation because it is a first and definitive conversion to God. As the *Rite of Penance* indicates:

> This victory is first brought to light in baptism where our fallen nature is crucified with Christ so that the body of sin may be destroyed and we may no longer be slaves to sin, but rise with Christ and live for God. For this reason the Church proclaims its faith in "the one baptism for the forgiveness of sins."

> Furthermore our Savior Jesus Christ, when he gave to his apostles and their successors power to forgive sins, instituted in his Church the sacrament of penance. Thus the faithful who fall into sin after baptism may be reconciled with God and renewed in grace. The Church "possesses both water and tears: the water of baptism, the tears of penance."[8]

The second sacrament of reconciliation is eucharist. The *Catechism of the Catholic Church* asserts this belief as does the constant teaching of the church.[9] The third century theologian, Origen, stressed the importance of the eucharist as the place for the forgiveness of sins. Origen's teaching was based on the many fellowship meals which Jesus had with sinners, thus teaching that the kingdom of God was a reconciling one and extended to all. The words "so that sins may be forgiven" were added to the eucharistic prayers in the early centuries of the church to reflect the insight that the eucharist is a real sacrament of reconciliation. The Fourth Lateran Council, in 1215, taught:

> The reception of eucharist is enough to efface all sins where no real malice is apparent. At the eucharistic meal, the church is assured that in the signs of remembrance, by the power of the Holy Spirit alone, the body and blood of reconciliation are truly present to it, not merely so that the church may fittingly praise God but above all so that it may participate once and for all in reconciliation.[10]

In addition to the inclusion of the words, "so that sins may be forgiven," to the eucharistic prayers, every eucharist includes, as part of the introductory rites, the rite of blessing and sprinkling holy water or the penitential rite. In the case of the rite of sprinkling holy water, the assembly calls to mind the water and grace of baptism, and prays:

> May almighty God cleanse us of our sins, and through the eucharist we celebrate make us worthy to sit at his table in his heavenly kingdom.[11]

In the case of the penitential rite, the presider invites the assembly to call to mind their sins and to repent of them in silence. After responding to the penitential invocations, the presider prays:

> May almighty God have mercy on us, forgive us our sins, and bring us to everlasting life.[12]

Many Catholics may not think of the eucharist as a means of reconciliation, due in large part to the emphasis the Council of Trent placed on the sacrament of reconciliation. Yet the history and teaching of the church, and the many references to reconciliation in the eucharistic prayers, clearly emphasize the reconciling nature of eucharist. From the early centuries of the church the eucharist was the ordinary sacrament of reconciliation in which Christians would find and grow in the reconciliation brought about by Christ.[13]

The third sacrament of reconciliation is the sacrament of anointing and viaticum. This sacrament is rooted in James 5:13–15, where the apostle says that if the sick person has committed any sins they will be forgiven through the prayer and anointing with oil of the community. We will discuss this sacrament in the next chapter.

The sacrament of reconciliation has been known by two other names—the sacrament of penance and the sacrament of confession. These three names—penance, confession and reconciliation—are a helpful key to the major historical developments in this sacrament.

The first Christian communities were convinced of the radical and definitive conversion required for baptism. They also seem to have been at a loss as to what to do with baptized Christians who engaged in public, scandalous sin. During the first hundred years of Christianity sinners were corrected and helped, but obdurate sinners were excluded from the church until they reformed their lives. In the second century, about 150, a man called Hermas seems to be the first to propose that postbaptismal sins can be forgiven, but only once. Here we have the beginnings of the sacrament of penance. At least four public, scandalous sins were the subject for this sacrament of penance: murder, adultery, heresy and apostasy. Penance was designed as a process to reinvigorate baptism. Similar in style to the stages of the catechumenate, the sinner needed a sponsor, a member of the community who walked with the sinner to encourage and support the penance required for reconciliation with God and the church. This process of canonical penance included the following: an interior admission of sin; a public admission of sin, usually in the presence of the bishop and accompanied by a sponsor, and enrollment in the "order of penitents"; a long period of doing penance, perhaps for as long as seven years, which included prayer, fasting and almsgiving, as well as exclusion from the eucharist; and, finally, reconciliation to the church through the bishop, often at Holy Thursday eucharist. This public, canonical penance required that the sinner demonstrate a real conversion and change of life similar to that required for baptism. The problem with canonical penance is that very few people made use of it for fear of never having another opportunity for forgiveness. For this reason many Christians delayed penance until the time of death.[14]

During the seventh to eleventh centuries, another form of reconciliation emerged in the church known as private confession. Christianity came to England, Ireland and Scotland principally through missionary monks. The Irish monks, especially, were accustomed to personal confession of their sins to another monk or to their abbot. The monks were assigned a penance for the specific sins they confessed. As these missionary monks brought Christianity to the British Isles, they encouraged

Catholics to confess their sins privately, do an assigned penance and celebrate reconciliation with God and the church through the absolution given by the monks. This system of the private confession of sins is testimony to the family-like relationship which the monks developed with people, and to the cultivation of a spiritual relationship between them. The monks enabled Catholics to examine their lives, discern patterns of sin and gave them encouragement and support to grow in faith. As this system of private confession developed, confession to a priest or bishop was required. To assist priests and bishops in selecting appropriate penances for people, penitential books were developed which listed every kind of sin with an appropriate penance. While the penitential books helped to regulate the kind of penances given, the practice of commutation caused serious problems for private confession; sometimes people were able to get others to substitute for them in doing penance or paying a fee to the church.

An important shift transpired as the sacrament of reconciliation moved from canonical penance to private confession. In the first centuries of the church the emphasis in canonical penance was on reconciliation of the sinner with God and the church. In the case of private confession the emphasis was on confession, contrition, satisfaction (doing penance) and absolution.[15] Private confession took hold in the church, however, and was reinforced in the theology of Thomas Aquinas and in the teachings of the Council of Trent.

The Second Vatican Council proposed a revision for the sacrament of penance, which focused on the importance of reconciliation. The purpose of the sacrament, according to Vatican II, is to reconcile sinners to God and the church, and to promote a life of conversion. In our current understanding, the sacrament of reconciliation is rooted in the lifelong journey of conversion, which is central to the baptismal commitment. Conversion can occur only within the context of Christian community, devoted to the ministry of reconciliation and to works of prayer, fasting and almsgiving. Sins may be secret or private, but they have communal implications. Just as one family member can bring disgrace or glory upon all who bear the family name, so too for the Christian. The sacrament of reconciliation is not so much a private event between the sinner and a priest, as a life-long journey of conversion within the context of the Christian community. The sacrament of reconciliation is integrally related to baptism and eucharist. Baptism is the initial and premier sacrament of reconciliation. Eucharist is the ordinary sacrament of reconciliation in that it enables the Christian to be nurtured in the life of conversion. Reconciliation deals with the concrete fact of sin and enables Christians to engage in a life of conversion.[16]

Theology and Celebration of the Rite

In responding to the Second Vatican Council's call for the revision of the *Rite of Penance,* the Congregation for Divine Worship published the *Rite of Penance* on 2 December 1973. The rationale given for the new *Rite of Penance* is noteworthy:

> The Church is solicitous in calling the faithful to continual conversion and renewal. It desires that the baptized who have sinned should acknowledge their sins against God and their neighbor and have heartfelt repentance for them, and it tries to prepare them to celebrate the sacrament of penance. For this reason the Church urges the faithful to attend penitential celebrations from time to time. This Congregation has therefore made regulations for such celebrations and has proposed examples or specimens which episcopal conferences may adapt to the needs of their own regions.[17]

Following the ancient custom of private confession in the church, the *Rite of Penance* indicates that the sacrament of penance includes four parts: contrition, confession, acts of penance (satisfaction), and absolution. Contrition includes the essential virtue of conversion—an honest recognition of sin, a heartfelt sorrow for the sin, and a sincere intention to lead a new life. Confession includes the articulation of the specific sins to the ordinary minister of the sacrament of penance, a priest or bishop. The confession of sin is made within the context of the mercy and compassion of God. Acts of penance (satisfaction) include the penitent's willingness to change sinful behaviors and to make reparation of injury. The acts of penance are suited to the personal condition of each penitent and to the kind and nature of sins confessed. Absolution includes the prayer of the minister of the sacrament, which assures the penitent that God receives with compassion, mercy and understanding the heartfelt intention of the sinner to live in the light of Jesus Christ. The prayer of absolution is a visible sign that God grants pardon to the sinner.[18] With hands extended over the penitent's head, the minister of the sacrament prays:

> God, the Father of mercies, through the death and resurrection of his Son has reconciled the world to himself and sent the Holy Spirit among us for the forgiveness of sins; through the ministry of the Church may God give you pardon and peace, and I absolve you from your sins in the name of the Father, and of the Son, + and of the Holy Spirit.[19]

The new *Rite of Penance* includes three forms: the rite for the reconciliation of individual penitents, the rite for reconciliation of several penitents with individual confession and absolution, and the rite for reconciliation of penitents with general confession and absolution. The rite also includes appendices which provide examples of penitential services for Lent and Advent, communal penitential celebrations, services for children, young people and the sick, and a sample form of an examination of conscience.

The rite most Catholics are familiar with, known as form one, is the rite for the reconciliation of individual penitents. This rite takes place in a confessional, which provides a place for the anonymous confession of sin, or a reconciliation room, a place which offers the penitent the option for the anonymous confession of sin or a face-to-face exchange between the penitent and the minister. Once the penitent enters the confessional or reconciliation room, the minister greets the penitent, who then makes the sign of the cross. The minister then invites the penitent to trust in the mercy, compassion and forgiveness of God, and then proclaims a short passage from the scriptures which proclaims God's mercy and calls people to conversion. The penitent then describes to the minister the sins for which he or she is sorry, making sure to give the number and kind of all serious, mortal sins. After this the minister offers helpful counsel and encouragement to the penitent and proposes an act of penance, appropriate to the penitent and the sins confessed. The penitent then expresses sorrow for sin by praying one of several prayers appropriate for this. After this prayer, the minister extends hands over the penitent and prays the prayer of absolution. The confession is concluded as the minister proclaims praise for God and dismisses the penitent.[20]

The second form of penance is the rite for reconciliation of several penitents with individual confession and absolution. Many Catholics are familiar with this form, which is often celebrated in parishes during Advent and Lent. This second form of penance is a wonderful example of the communal and ecclesial nature of sin and reconciliation; it provides Catholics with the opportunity to reflect on the social consequences of sin and the blessing of a community which encourages and supports members in living a life of conversion. This form of penance begins with a liturgy of the word. The community gathers in the usual place for worship and begins with the introductory rites, which may include song, a greeting from the presider, an introduction to the nature of this particular worship experience and an opening prayer. The community then participates in a liturgy of the word, which may include several readings, including a responsorial psalm, a homily and an examination of conscience. The readings selected usually reflect the biblical call to conversion, the reconciling nature of Christ's passion, death and resurrection, and the mercy, compassion and forgiveness of God. The community then celebrates the rite of reconciliation, which usually includes a general confession of sin, a litany of reconciliation, the Lord's Prayer, individual confession and absolution, a proclamation of praise for God's mercy and a concluding prayer of thanksgiving. The rite concludes with a blessing and dismissal.[21] This form of penance is a communal celebration of reconciliation; however, sufficient priests must be available for the individual confessions and absolution.

The third form of penance, the one Catholics are probably least familiar with, is the rite of reconciliation of several penitents with general confession and absolution. The *Catechism of the Catholic Church* indicates that this form is used only in cases of grave necessity, such as the imminent danger of death or the lack of a sufficient number of ministers. The diocesan bishop is always the judge of when this third form of penance may be celebrated.[22] This third form is similar to the second form, and begins with the usual introductory rites and a liturgy of the word. The celebration then proceeds to general confession, which includes an instruction from the minister on the necessity of general absolution in this particular circumstance and the obligation the individual penitents have to make a private confession of all serious, mortal sins at a later date. The community participates in a general confession of sins, a litany of reconciliation or song, and the Lord's Prayer. The minister then extends hands over all the penitents and prays the prayer of absolution. The rite then concludes with a song, a blessing and a dismissal.[23]

All three forms of the *Rite of Penance* are designed to enable Catholics to reconcile themselves to God and to the church, to deal with the concrete fact of sin and to engage in a life of conversion.

Pastoral Challenges

Recent scholarship suggests that the documents of the Second Vatican Council reflect three twentieth-century theological trends, especially in regard to the *Rite of Penance:* 1) penance/reconciliation is social and ecclesial in its nature as well as its effects; 2) penance is an act of ecclesial worship (as are all sacraments); 3) the deepest meaning of penance is conversion which goes beyond ritual to the whole of the Christian life.[24] This theology presents the challenges Catholics face in celebrating the sacrament of reconciliation. The first challenge in celebrating this sacrament is to recognize the social and ecclesial nature and effect of sin and reconciliation. North American culture is pervaded with the cult of the personal and private. We are sometimes obsessed with our individual rights and freedoms to the exclusion of our social responsibilities. The *Rite of Penance* challenges us to recognize the social and ecclesial effects of our sin and our reconciliation. Sin slowly destroys individuals and the community. Likewise reconciliation slowly restores to wholeness individuals and the community. The new *Rite of Penance* challenges Catholics to balance individual rights and freedoms with our social and ecclesial responsibilities.

The second challenge in celebrating this sacrament is to recognize the *Rite of Penance* as an act of worship. For too long Catholics have viewed penance as a private affair between priest and penitent, in which the emphasis was on the private confession of sin and absolution from the priest. In fact, penance is an act of worship, which includes praise and thanks to God for his mercy, compassion and forgiveness; a celebration of the word of God, which encourages and supports the community of faith in its journey of conversion; and the prayer of the church. The new *Rite of Penance* challenges Catholics to face the dual reality that we are not only sinful individuals but a sinful community. Only within the context of the community, gathered around the table of God's word and in a spirit of praise and thanksgiving to God, can individuals celebrate the reconciliation Christ entrusted to the church.

The third challenge in celebrating the new *Rite of Penance* is the gospel truth that baptism includes repentance for the forgiveness of sins. Through the sacrament of penance Catholics seek to restore their relationship with both God and the church by engaging in a lifelong journey of conversion.

> The revitalization of confession and reconciliation is important because it takes up the call of continuous conversion seen as the constant dynamic of the Christian life, begun in baptism and fulfilled at the Lord's table. To take up that task together for the sake of truly pastoral care could go a long way not only toward further liturgical renewal, but toward our own renewal as well.[25]

Reconciliation occurs through the celebration of the *Rite of Penance,* but it pervades the whole of life as Catholics walk the journey of faith. The new *Rite of Penance* challenges Catholics to be reconciled with the church, in the home, the neighborhood, the school, the workplace, indeed in all the world.

The new *Rite of Penance* challenges Catholics to continual renewal of their baptismal faith and to humble submission to the process of reconciliation. The first and premier sacrament of reconciliation is baptism, the foundation and touchstone of the Christian life. Reconciliation is a lifelong journey of conversion which includes the ability to recognize sin, to forgive oneself, to reconcile with others, especially those injured by sin, and to reconcile oneself with the church.

Summary

The sacrament of reconciliation is the usual way Catholics celebrate the forgiveness of postbaptismal sins through a life devoted to conversion, contrition, confession, satisfaction and absolution. Reconciliation reinvigorates the grace of baptism and enables Catholics to walk in the light of Jesus Christ as they celebrate the unconditional love and mercy of God within the context of a healing and forgiving community of faith. Gathered in sacred assembly, enlightened and challenged by the word of God, Catholics celebrate through worship and prayer the mercy, compassion and forgiveness of God, and courageously, with heartfelt sorrow, confess their sins and pledge to engage in acts of penance as a visible sign of their commitment to a lifelong journey of conversion and reconciliation.

Questions for Reflection and Discussion

1. How is the sacrament of reconciliation rooted in the ministry of Jesus?

2. Why are baptism and eucharist considered sacraments of reconciliation?

3. What is the origin of private confession of sin?

4. In what ways do the various rites of reconciliation complement each other?

8

Anointing of the Sick and Viaticum

*M*argaret was dying. Everybody knew it. Margaret knew it best of all. She had been a very active member of her parish. For years she had taken great care of the decorations for the various seasons of the year. She had a wonderful eye for making the sanctuary beautiful. She never overdid anything. The people loved her. The whole parish saw the effects of her cancer. It was no surprise that the time had come. Many were finding it really difficult to let her go.

Father Bill finished the morning mass and was still taking off his vestments when he was surrounded by Margaret's friends. Some were weeping. All were very concerned. They wanted to make sure that Father Bill knew of Margaret's condition. Father Bill told them that yes, he was aware of her condition. He intended to go to the hospital right after mass. He came out of the sacristy and realized that almost no one had left the church. Most were standing in groups looking very serious; some were crying. Father Bill knew what was happening and asked everyone to come together.

He began: "We know that our dear friend Margaret is dying. I know how bad you feel about this. Really, we have all known that this day would come. I need you to help me out. I am going to the hospital now to anoint her and I need you to pray with me so that I can do a good job for her."

Everyone knelt down. Father Bill talked to them a bit about anointing. He told them how important the sick are to the whole church. He asked them to pray in silence that the comforting hand of the Lord would be upon their dear friend. He told them that he would be bringing Margaret communion and that they could participate by remembering her in prayer for the next hour. He explained that Margaret had seemed to make her peace with her own dying and had told him how much she wanted to be with the Lord. They had to let her go free.

Father Bill then did something that really moved this morning congregation. He explained that one of the essential elements of the rite of the anointing of the sick was the prayer of the church for comfort. He told them about the soothing qualities of the olive oil and how he intended to try to comfort Margaret with prayer, the laying on of hands, and the use of soothing oil. He then asked them to stand and extend a hand over him in silent prayer. He would then leave them and go to Margaret, empowered by the prayers of her friends.

Father Bill rushed off to the hospital, feeling better about the sacrament he was about to minister than he ever had before. He arrived at Margaret's room very anxious to share with her the love and affection of her many friends from the parish. He was about to walk in, but stopped when he heard someone inside talking. Assuming Margaret was being attended to by medical personnel, he began to walk away. Then suddenly he recognized the voice. It was Gail. Gail was Margaret's closest friend. They often worked in church together. Father Bill came close and was just amazed at what he saw and heard.

Gail took a cool towel and placed it on Margaret's forehead. She then took the lotion that all patients get in hospitals and began to apply it to Margaret's arms and legs. Gail kept telling her not to be afraid and how beautiful it would be to see Jesus. Father Bill was deeply moved. He thought to himself how Gail was actually doing the anointing that he had come to do. Anointing had to do with the people of God taking care of each other, and there was Gail doing exactly that.

Gail finally looked up and was startled to see her priest there. She excused herself and backed away from Margaret. Father Bill said, "No, please continue. I will pray with you."

Gail continued to comfort Margaret while Father Bill said the prayers of the church for a dying member. When it came time for the anointing, Margaret looked up briefly and said with a smile, "Thanks, I'm ready."

Origins

After reading the gospels, especially Mark, it is readily apparent that Jesus had great compassion and care for the sick and the dying. Jesus was concerned with the whole person and spent much of his ministry caring for many sick people. The first chapters of Mark's gospel are a good example of Jesus' special care for the sick. In these chapters Jesus cures a demoniac, Simon's mother-in-law, a leper, a paralytic, a man with a withered hand, and many others who were in some kind of physical distress.[1] Jesus' healing ministry is also attested to in the other gospels: the healing of a centurion's servant (Mt 8:5–13); the healing of the daughter of an official and the woman with a hemorrhage (Mt 9:18–26); the healing of a boy with a demon (Lk 9:37–43); the cure of a crippled woman on the Sabbath (Lk 13:10–17); the cleansing of ten lepers (Lk 17:11–19); the man born blind (Jn 9:1–41); the raising of Lazarus (Jn 11:1–44); and many others. The sacrament of the anointing of the sick and viaticum is rooted in the ministry of Jesus Christ.

The *Catechism of the Catholic Church* teaches that the sacrament of anointing is rooted in the human experience of sickness, suffering and death. These experiences often cause some of the most difficult pain and anguish we will ever experience. Sickness and death confront us with our limitations and our powerlessness. While suffering often enables us to grow in wholeness as persons, it can also lead us to despair and to question the existence and the care of God for all of us.[2] Sickness and death are part of the mystery of what it means to be human.

The sacrament of anointing, rooted in the human experience of sickness and death, is essentially part of the lifelong journey of Christian conversion. This mystery was first encountered in the sacraments of initiation, when we died to sin and rose with Christ to new life. Just as the sacraments of initiation—baptism, confirmation and eucharist—form the beginning of our Christian life, so too the sacraments of penance, anointing and eucharist form the end of our Christian life.[3] Sickness and death challenge Christians to unite themselves to the passion, death and resurrection of Jesus Christ, and to integrate the mystery of suffering and death into their ordinary human experience.

The sacrament of the anointing of the sick and viaticum has traditionally been rooted in the apostolic ministry of the church, especially in the Letter of James 5:14–15:

Is anyone among you sick? He should summon the presbyters of the church, and they should pray over him and
anoint [him] with oil in the name of the Lord, and the prayer
of faith will save the sick person, and the Lord will raise him
up. If he has committed any sins, he will be forgiven.

This passage is testimony to the fact that the followers of Jesus
took his ministry to the sick and dying very seriously. Mark's
gospel tells us that Jesus specifically commissioned the disciples,
in a postresurrection appearance, to "lay hands on the sick, and
they will recover."[4] Matthew's gospel, in the parable of the judgment of the nations, lists the visitation and care of the sick as
one of many practices of those who will enter the kingdom of
God.[5] Jesus' preferential option for the sick and the dying was
such an essential and integral part of his ministry that Christians
quickly took up this ministry, as attested to in many places in the
New Testament.

Historical Developments

While the ministry of Jesus and the Letter of James give
clear testimony to Christians' concern and care for the sick and
the dying, there is little commentary about the sacrament of
anointing for approximately seven hundred years. This is probably due, in part, to the individual and private nature of sickness
and death. James 5:15–16 clearly indicates a practice of the early
church in caring for the sick, a practice which included the presence of a Christian leader, prayers, anointing with oil, the forgiveness of sin, and the attempt to restore the sick to both
physical and spiritual health.[6] While we would like to know much
more about this sacrament from these early centuries, there is
simply not much information available. In the first century, Hippolytus describes the bishop consecrating the oil used to anoint
the sick. In the fifth century, Pope Innocent I, referring to James
5:15–16, calls anointing a sacrament of the sick and says that
bishops, priests and all Christians may anoint those who are sick
and dying with the oil of the sick.[7] According to Pope Innocent,
Christians could anoint themselves or anoint one another. They

could apply the oil of the sick externally to their body, or drink it. While the bishop or priest was the ordinary minister of this sacrament, baptized Christians also participated in celebrating the sacrament of anointing.[8]

A major shift in emphasis in the sacrament of anointing took place at the beginning of the ninth century. Under the influence of the emperor Charlemagne, who imposed Roman liturgical and disciplinary practices throughout the new Roman empire, the sacrament of anointing became restricted to those who were dying. By the end of the twelfth century, anointing becomes extreme unction (last anointing), the sacrament for the dying.[9] In the fifteenth and sixteenth centuries, at the Council of Florence and the Council of Trent, this revised understanding of anointing as the sacrament for the dying was confirmed and enhanced. These councils stressed the importance of Christians visiting the sick and caring for them, but also clearly taught that the priest was the proper minister of the sacrament, which most often included penance, and that this sacrament of extreme unction prepared people for death.[10] This theology and practice of the sacrament lasted until the twentieth century.

In the liturgical studies which preceded the Second Vatican Council, some theologians viewed anointing as a preparation for death, while others viewed it as a sacrament for the sick and viaticum as the last sacrament. Viaticum, which literally means "food for the journey," was taken up in the reforms of Vatican II. The *Constitution on the Sacred Liturgy,* no. 68, calls viaticum the last sacrament to be administered to the dying. The *Dogmatic Constitution on the Church,* no. 11, says that the sacrament of anointing, celebrated by the priest, and including anointing with the oil of the sick, the laying on of hands and the prayer of the church, is for those who are seriously sick and those who are in danger of death from sickness and old age.[11] This renewed understanding of the sacrament of anointing and viaticum was promulgated by Pope Paul VI on 30 November 1972, when the new rite was issued entitled *Pastoral Care of the Sick: Rites of Anointing and Viaticum.*[12]

Theology and Celebration of the Rite

Pastoral Care of the Sick is a rather comprehensive and thorough approach to care of the sick and dying. Part 1, "Pastoral Care of the Sick," includes rituals for visits to the sick, including sick children; communion for the sick, including communion in a hospital or institution; and anointing of the sick, both within and outside of mass, and in a hospital or institution. Part 2, "Pastoral Care of the Dying," includes rituals for viaticum, both within and outside of mass; prayers for the dying and the dead; a continuous rite of penance and anointing; rites for emergencies; Christian initiation for the dying; and an appendix of scripture passages which may be used in any of these situations.

In the general introduction the theology of the rites of anointing and viaticum is presented. Suffering and illness are situated within the context of ordinary human experience and within the specific context of Christian life. The church, following the example of Christ, cares for and prays with the sick. The sick, also following the example of Christ, serve as a reminder to the church of our human mortality and our radical need for the redemption which Christ's suffering, death and resurrection brought us.[13]

The anointing of the sick consists in the laying on of hands by a priest, the prayers of the church, and the anointing with the oil of the sick. The sacrament strengthens the sick to fight against illness and return to physical health. "If necessary, the sacrament also provides the sick person with the forgiveness of sins and the completion of Christian penance."[14] Anyone suffering from serious illness and elderly people may be anointed, and the sacrament may be repeated.

Viaticum for the dying, the reception of the eucharist prior to death, is focused on the mystery of the death of Christ and his passage to God. The continuous rite includes the celebration of penance, anointing and eucharist. This rite is especially helpful for those who are near death and yet well enough to participate in the prayers. When the sick person is not able to participate, a shorter rite is provided.

Pastoral Care of the Sick emphasizes the fact that ministry to the sick is the responsibility of the entire church.

> This ministry is the common responsibility of all Christians, who should visit the sick, remember them in prayer, and celebrate the sacraments with them. The family and friends of the sick, doctors and others who care for them, and priests with pastoral responsibilities have a particular share in this ministry of comfort. Through words of encouragement and faith they can help the sick to unite themselves with the sufferings of Christ for the good of God's people.[15]

The church's ministry to the sick and dying is thus not a private affair between the priest and the sick/dying person, but rather a communal act of care and worship.

The rite for anointing the sick consists of an introductory rite, an instruction, a penitential rite, a liturgy of the word and homily, the liturgy of anointing, the Lord's Prayer, communion and a concluding rite. After greeting the sick and others present for the rite, the priest addresses those present and reminds them of Christ's ministry to the sick and the teaching of the Letter of James. The rite then proceeds to a penitential rite in which the sick petition God for mercy and forgiveness. In the liturgy of the word, appropriate selections from scripture are proclaimed which focus on suffering, sickness and the need Christians have for the redemptive healing of Christ. The priest is encouraged to give a brief homily, relating the readings to the needs of the sick and those who are caring for them. In the liturgy of anointing the priest lays hands on the head of the sick person in silence, and then anoints the head and the hands of the sick with these words:

> Through this holy anointing may the Lord in his love and mercy help you with the grace of the Holy Spirit. May the Lord who frees you from sin save you and raise you up.[16]

The rite then proceeds to the Lord's Prayer, the reception of communion, and a blessing and dismissal.

When the condition of the sick permits, anointing occurs with the context of eucharist. Many parishes schedule communal anointings of the sick several times during the year and make special efforts to provide transportation and hospitality for the sick during these celebrations. When anointing occurs within eucharist, there is a special greeting and reception of the sick during the introductory rites. After the liturgy of the word, the actual laying on of hands and anointing with the oil of the sick take place. A special preface is provided for the eucharistic celebration, including special intercessions for eucharistic prayers I, II and III.[17]

Pastoral Care of the Dying provides various rites to comfort and strengthen those who are near death, and emphasizes trust in Christ's promise of eternal life. The introduction to this part of the rite emphasizes the responsibility of the entire Christian community to pray for and with the dying.[18] The rite for viaticum includes: the introductory rites; an instruction; the penitential rite; the liturgy of the word and homily; the liturgy of viaticum; a concluding prayer, a blessing and the sign of peace. After the priest greets the dying and those gathered for prayer with them, he gives the following brief instruction:

> My brothers and sisters, before our Lord Jesus Christ passed from this world to return to the Father, he left us the sacrament of his body and blood. When the hour comes for us to pass from this life and join him, he strengthens us with this food for our journey and comforts us by this pledge of his resurrection.[19]

The penitential rite follows, in which the dying seek God's mercy and forgiveness. During the liturgy of the word, appropriate passages from scripture are proclaimed which focus on the mystery of death and Christ's promise of eternal life. The priest then gives a brief homily, suited to the circumstances of the dying and their family and friends. During the liturgy of viaticum, all present pray the Lord's Prayer and receive communion. When the priest gives communion to the dying, the form for viaticum is used: "Jesus Christ is the food of our journey; he calls us to the heavenly table." [20] The rite concludes with a prayer, a blessing and the sign of peace.

The continuous rite of penance, anointing and viaticum is very similar to the rite just described, except that after the greeting and instruction, the sacrament of penance is celebrated. If the sick person is not able to celebrate the sacrament in the usual way, a general confession of sin is permitted.

Pastoral Care of the Sick is testimony to the church's ancient practice and tradition of love and care for the sick and dying. The rite clearly focuses on the healing ministry of Jesus Christ, the apostolic practice mentioned in the Letter of James and the history of the practice of this sacrament in the church. As the *Catechism of the Catholic Church* teaches, this sacrament enables those who are sick to experience the healing power of Christ in body and soul. This sacrament unites the sick with the ministry, passion, death and resurrection of Christ. Anointing and viaticum are ecclesial acts of worship which strengthen and sanctify the community of faith. Viaticum prepares the dying for the passage from this life to the next, in the sure and certain hope of the resurrection of the just.[21]

Pastoral Challenges

The sacrament of anointing of the sick and viaticum challenges Christians to deal with and celebrate one of the central and most challenging mysteries of what it means to be human—the mystery of sickness, suffering and death. The ministry of Jesus, the apostolic tradition of the Letter of James and the tradition of the church challenge us to recognize sickness and death as inevitable human experiences. Few people go through life without sickness; all people face death. The first challenge is to integrate these experiences and to seek to find the meaning and value of these experiences. Sickness and death cause us to ask questions such as: What is the meaning of sickness and suffering? Why death at an early age or in old age? Is there a purpose to suffering and sickness? Why me? Why now? Sickness and death raise more questions than we have answers for. Christians believe that the redemptive passion, death and resurrection of Jesus Christ teach us that sickness and suffering lead us to view life from a new and different perspective. Death is a final "rite of passage" which challenges us to focus our life on the values, attitudes and beliefs of Jesus Christ and his proclamation of the kingdom of God. Anointing is the completion of our Christian life and marks our final conformity to following in the footsteps of Christ. Baptism marks and seals us at the beginning of our Christian life, confirmation seals and strengthens us for the journey of our life, eucharist provides us with the ongoing nourishment necessary to witness to the presence of Christ in ourselves and our world, and anointing and viaticum prepare us for our final passage from this life to life forever with God.

The second challenge of anointing and viaticum is to integrate those who are sick and dying into the community of faith. This is quite a challenge for a society that increasingly isolates the sick and dying from the rest of us. Hospitals, nursing homes and other institutions provide protective barriers to separate the sick from the healthy, the dying from the living. Health care professionals take care of the sick and dying, and the rest of us can feel complacent in the feeling that someone else is taking care of all of their needs. Our human experience teaches us that there is more to disease than the physical pathology involved in a given sickness—cancer or AIDS, for example. There is also the experience of being sick, the illness, which includes the struggle to find meaning in pain and fear, to draw out some good from the experience. All people know they are going to die some day, but illness makes this knowledge concrete. Anointing and viaticum challenge the entire Christian community to follow the example of Jesus and seek out and care for those who are sick and dying, and to pray with and for them. This ministry is the common responsibility of all Christians—family and friends, doctors and other health care professionals, and the entire church. The sick and dying will experience the healing power of Christ through the prayers and rituals of the church and the care, love and concern of the baptized.

The third challenge in celebrating anointing and viaticum is to recognize this sacrament, like all of the sacraments, as an act of communal worship. *Pastoral Care of the Sick* includes rituals for visits to the sick, communion for the sick and for anointing of the sick and viaticum. The actual rituals presume the presence of sick and dying people, a priest, family, friends and members of the parish community. The various liturgies include introductory rites, a liturgy of the word and homily, a liturgy of anointing and viaticum, the Lord's Prayer and communion, and a blessing and dismissal. Additionally, these liturgies may be celebrated in hospitals and other institutions, and sometimes in the parish church. Only within the context of a community of faith, presided over by a priest and gathered around the table of God's word in a spirit of humility, praise and thanksgiving to God, can the sick and dying, indeed the entire church, encounter the redemptive passion, death and resurrection of Jesus Christ.

The fourth challenge in celebrating anointing and viaticum is to select, train and commission members of the parish community to engage in the ministry to the sick and dying. *Pastoral Care of the Sick,* as we have already indicated, proposes this ministry as the common responsibility of all Christians. However, not every Christian possesses the skills, theology or personality necessary to provide care and support to the sick and dying. Recent advances in medicine and psychology lead us to believe that sick and dying people have specific and unique needs, and that those who care for them need specific training. Many dioceses and parishes provide training programs for persons who engage in ministry to the sick and dying. If this challenge is to be met, then parish communities will select, train and commission people who know and understand the church's teaching on sickness and death.

Pastoral Care of the Sick: Rites of Anointing and Viaticum challenges Catholics to embrace the struggle of the journey of baptismal faith and to accept sickness, suffering and death, trusting in Christ's promised strength, healing and eternal life. Just as the sacraments of initiation begin our journey of conversion, anointing and viaticum initiate us into the mystery of suffering and prepare us for the final passage from this life to life forever with God.

Summary

The sacrament of anointing and viaticum is the usual way Catholics encounter the healing and redemptive presence of Christ amidst the inevitable pain, suffering and death which come to us all. Rooted in the ministry of Jesus, the apostolic ministry of the Letter of James, and the tradition of the church, this sacrament enables the church to take up in every generation Jesus' special ministry to the sick and dying, and empowers the sick to experience the kind of conversion St. Paul speaks about: "My grace is sufficient for you, for power is made perfect in weakness."[22] Through anointing and viaticum Christians participate in the dying and rising with Christ, first celebrated in baptism. In the laying on of hands, the prayer of the church and the anointing with the oil of the sick, Christians participate in the saving work of Christ.

Questions for Reflection and Discussion

1. How is the sacrament of the anointing of the sick rooted in the human experience of suffering and death?

2. Why is the ministry to the sick the responsibility of the whole church?

3. What are the essential elements of the rite of anointing?

4. What role do the sick and dying play in the community of faith?

5. How is the healing and redemptive presence of Christ effective in the rite of anointing?

THE SACRAMENTS
OF COMMITMENT

✝ ✝ ✝

9

Marriage

*C*B had been called CB for so long that he had just about forgotten why he was called that. He remembered with a smile how it had come about. He and Helen met when they were in high school. They fell in love, as teenagers will, with incredible intensity. They just enjoyed each other's company. It wasn't long before they began to talk about how they would want to be together all the days of their lives. Helen was very affectionate. CB was stalky and practical. When CB would let the matter-of-facts of life dampen his spirit, Helen would always hug him and call him her "cuddly bear." CB, being really embarrassed when Helen called him that in public, asked her to stop calling him "cuddly bear," and thus he was named CB, and no one was supposed to know that under his practical, no-nonsense demeanor was truly a cuddly bear.

They were inseparable. Many times their parents complained that they were too intense and perhaps they needed to meet other people. Perhaps they were too young to be getting so deeply involved. Neither would listen to the advice given them. They began very early on to talk about marriage and children and growing up together. CB had always thought that the only practical thing to do was to get married. However, it was Helen who convinced him that they should wait until they were more mature. This waiting was the most difficult thing CB had ever done.

They decided that they would marry when they both turned twenty-one. The only problem with that was it gave CB a lot of time to worry about the consequences of being married. Would he be able to provide for Helen? If they had children, would he be a good father? What if he got attracted to someone else? Could he be faithful forever? The questions and the fears began to increase as the months and years unfolded toward their wedding day. When he would get particularly worked up, Helen would take him by the hand and remind him gently, "You are my

CB and I can't live without you." CB would sigh and smile and realize that he couldn't live without Helen either.

They married. They had five children. They became successful. They struggled, worried, fought, and from time to time, had a really good time together. The years of their marriage passed like the pages of a good book. They were good people. He was practical. She was sensitive. They were preparing to celebrate their golden wedding anniversary.

Months before the day, CB became really fascinated with the idea of marking fifty years together. After dinner he would sit before the TV and muse about the many events that made the story of their marriage. From time to time he would get nostalgic and sometimes melancholy as he would remember the difficult times. Helen would just reach out to him and touch his arm and say, "Remember, you are my CB." That was always enough.

CB wanted a big celebration. He wanted all his friends and all of his children and grandchildren to come together for a big party. He was successful. He could afford it. Helen refused. She said, "I'm an old lady now. I don't want everyone looking at me." She suggested that they just go to mass together on the anniversary day and have the priest give them a blessing. That would be enough. She would make him a wonderful breakfast afterward.

CB loved her more after fifty years than he did when they first made marriage vows. He wanted to do something special. He wanted to be impractical and romantic. Helen refused the party. She also refused his offer to buy her a new ring. "I have held on to this ring for fifty years. I look at it every day and remember the promises I made to you. I don't want to be looking at any other ring."

CB wanted desperately to do something special for their anniversary day. He finally settled on doing something they had done their whole married life. For birthdays and holidays, on sick days and celebration days, he would buy her a card from the card shop. He always liked the pictures on the outside and never paid much attention to the greeting inside. They were always good. He figured he had bought a thousand cards over the years. He would choose a card he liked and often without reading the sentiments inside would sign it, "Your CB."

CB knew that Helen would accept a card from him for the anniversary. He would pick the perfect card and sign it and give it to her at the door of the church where they married fifty years earlier.

He spent a long time at the card store. He was surprised at how many choices there were. He looked for the most beautiful card that would express his love. After a long time he chose a card that pictured a mature couple holding hands and walking down a country road. The outside of the card said, "Beloved, our journey together has been wonderful!" CB thought it was perfect.

As he prepared for bed on the night before his anniversary, CB remembered that he needed to sign the card. He left Helen in the bedroom and went to the kitchen. He took a glass of milk and looked at his card for a long time. He remembered a lot and cried a little. He finally opened the card to sign it and was horrified. The card was blank. Nothing, no greeting, no romantic words were written there. He panicked. What could he do at the last moment? Finally, he took up a pen and wrote–

My dearest Helen,
Take me by the arm today because with you I have never been afraid. I thank God for you every day of my life. I cannot imagine life without you. I promise you that I will take your arm tomorrow and God will bless me as he has done for these many years.

With all my love,
Your CB

Origins

Marriage is as old as the human race, but its precise origins and various forms are still the subject of historical investigation. "And whether marriage began with promiscuity or fidelity, monogamy or polygamy, matriarchy or patriarchy is a historical question that likewise may never be answered."[1] Historical records indicate that marriage was a well-established part of all cultures, though it had a variety of forms as diverse as the cultures in which it existed. Like the other sacraments, marriage has its origins in the ministry of Jesus. Marriage was regarded as a sacrament in the early history of Christianity, though it was not until the thirteenth century that marriage was regarded as a sacrament like the other sacraments. For many centuries civil governments regulated marriage. With the collapse of the

Roman empire Christian bishops began to control marriage, and developed liturgical ceremonies to celebrate marriage that eventually became universal throughout the church.[2]

Jesus understood marriage within the context of the Old Testament, especially the Genesis creation stories. In the first story of creation, God created humankind on the sixth day. Men and women are seen as the pinnacle of God's creation because they are created in the very image of God and given dominion over all of creation. It is within the context of a relationship of love and fidelity that God instructs man and woman to bear children. In the second story of creation, God formed man, and subsequently woman, out of the clay of the earth and breathed into them the breath of life. This story portrays man and woman as sharing in the very life of God. God is as intimate to humankind as the air they breathe. With God they live; without God they die.[3] The *Code of Canon Law* summarizes this understanding of marriage in the following way:

> The matrimonial covenant, by which a man and a woman establish between themselves a partnership of the whole of life, is by its nature ordered toward the good of the spouses and the procreation and education of offspring; this covenant between baptized persons has been raised by Christ the Lord to the dignity of a sacrament.[4]

The *Catechism of the Catholic Church* indicates that the scriptures are pervaded with a theology and understanding of marriage, as ordained by God, from the first book of Genesis to the last book, Revelation.[5]

While the New Testament does not contain a complete theology of marriage, Jesus did have some things to say about it. Jesus denounced divorce and remarriage, and thus stood in opposition to such practices in the Judaism of his day.[6] In the sermon on the mount Jesus provided detailed instructions to his disciples on a variety of topics and issues.

> Jesus' standards of morality were high, his call to perfection was revolutionary, and he often presented his teachings in radical, absolute statements. In his "sermon on the mount," for example, Jesus proclaimed that anger is a capital offense,

that lust is equivalent to adultery, that swearing oaths is wrong, and that loving one's enemies is right. No less forth-rightly he commanded his followers to do good only in secret, to renounce wealth, to avoid judging people, and to cut off any part of their body that sins (Matthew 5–7). In this manner, then, Jesus also preached an ideal of lasting fidelity in marriage, and he proposed it as a norm for all those who heeded his call to moral perfection.[7]

In a very real sense, the sacrament of marriage has its origins in Jesus' teachings on discipleship, fidelity and love of neighbor. Christian marriage implies a conversion to the Lord Jesus Christ. It is patterned after the relationship of discipleship, a lifelong journey of learning and conversion, living and dying in imitation of Jesus Christ. It is no accident that John's gospel presents Jesus' first miracle at the wedding feast of Cana. Jesus' presence at the wedding confirms the goodness of marriage and the fact that through marriage men and women become a sign of his presence to the world.[8]

Marriage as a way to discipleship, fidelity and love of neighbor is a familiar theme in Paul's letters. In Ephesians, Paul instructs husbands and wives to love one another just as Christ loves the church. Paul sees marriage as a "great mystery" which reflects the relationship between Christ and the church.[9] As married people develop a lifelong relationship of fidelity to one another, they are called to model their relationship on that between Jesus and his disciples, and through their community with one another to serve those most in need.

Historical Developments

In the ancient Greek and Roman worlds, which profoundly influenced Christianity, marriage was a local family affair, which sometimes included religious rites. Fathers arranged the marriage of their daughters, selecting their prospective husbands, in order to protect the family name and wealth. At this stage of history, in a patriarchal society, women were subject first to their fathers and then to their husbands. As the Roman world became more centralized, various customs and laws governed marriage.

While no marriage contract existed, marriages were forbidden between a citizen and a slave, between a citizen and a foreigner, and between persons of certain degrees of kinship. Divorce and polygamy were tolerated. In the absence of marriage contracts and formal, public rituals, only the mutual consent of the parties to the marriage was required.[10]

Ancient Israel was, for a time, influenced by the Greek and Roman models of marriage. Israel tolerated polygamy and divorce. However, after the exile the Jewish prophets, believing that the exile was the result of Israel's infidelity to God, urged husbands and wives to be faithful to one another as a sign of their faithfulness to God.[11] Jesus picks up on this theme of fidelity in marriage.

Christian marriages were externally not much different from other marriages. During the first four centuries, the fathers of the church and some councils explicitly stated that Christians marry according to local civil custom. The mutual consent of the man and woman was all that was needed. The fathers of the church saw marriage as a duty to society in that the very nature of marriage was to produce children and continue God's creation of the world by providing a future for the world. By the end of the fourth century, a priest or bishop began to offer a blessing to the newly married couple and to take an active role in the civil ceremony, though this was not required. Perhaps the most influential theologian during this period was Augustine, who taught that marriage accomplished three goals: fidelity, offspring and sacrament. Marriage enables a man and a woman to be mutually faithful and loving. Marriage enables children to be accepted as a loving gift from God; mothers and fathers nurture them with affection and educate them in the Christian faith. Marriage enables husbands and wives to participate in the life of God through their participation in the mystery of Christ. Husbands and wives are signs to the world of the love and faithfulness of Christ.[12]

Gradually, during the Middle Ages, marriage was confirmed as a sacrament. In 1208, Pope Innocent III called marriage a sacrament. This teaching was reaffirmed in 1274 by the Second Council of Lyons, in 1439 by the Council of Florence, and in 1563 at the Council of Trent, which also required that

Catholic marriages take place in the presence of a priest. The Council of Trent, which responded to the Protestant Reformation, firmly established marriage as a sacrament and the church's authority over marriage, and rejected divorce. The Council of Trent taught that from then on, all marriages were valid only if they were celebrated before a priest and two witnesses. The reformers, while believing in the sacredness of marriage, rejected it as a sacrament, and thus the church's authority over marriage, and approved divorce.[13] During the Middle Ages marriage was viewed as a contract, an exchange of rights and duties between husbands and wives, especially in regard to the procreation of children. But this contractual approach to marriage included an understanding of marriage as a vehicle for holiness. Reflecting the teachings of the New Testament on marriage, theologians and church councils taught that marriage was indissoluble because it reflected Christ's covenant of love with the church. Just as Christ urged fidelity in every area of life, so too, married couples were to be faithful to one another.

During the period from the Council of Trent to Vatican II, this understanding of marriage experienced many challenges. As major parts of the world moved from agriculture to industry, and as life became much more complex, marriage moved away from its roots in communal responsibility to become a matter of personal choice and individual fulfillment. Marriage became a very private affair. Theologians began to study once again the early roots of marriage within Christianity, and by the time of Vatican II several important shifts in the Catholic understanding of marriage occurred. First, marriage is described as a community of life and love, not simply as a contract. Second, marriage is not defined in terms of primary and secondary ends, in which the procreation of children is always more important than the mutual love of husband and wife.

> Hence, while not making the other ends of marriage of less value, the true practice of conjugal love, and the whole nature of family life resulting from it, tend to dispose the spouses to cooperate courageously with the love of the Creator and Savior, who through them day by day expands and enriches His own family.[14]

Third, marriage involves the mutual consent and exchange of love between husbands and wives. Married couples enter into a lifelong journey of conversion and mutual growth in love. Fourth, marriage involves faith—it is a sacrament, an act of worship, an expression of faith, a sign of the church's unity and a witness to the presence of Christ.[15]

As the *Catechism of the Catholic Church* teaches, Vatican II's theology of marriage emphasizes marriage as a covenant in which husbands and wives join together in an intimate communion of life and love, which reflects the union of Christ and the church. Marriage is based on the mutual consent of the parties, and on their willingness to give themselves to one another in unity and lifelong faithfulness. Marriage as sacrament is a public act of worship on the part of the church, which must include a liturgical celebration before a priest, two witnesses and the assembly of the church. Marriage and family life constitute "the domestic church" in that the home is the place where children are nurtured in the faith and learn the Christian virtues, especially charity.[16]

Theology and Celebration of the Rite

The revised *Rite of Marriage* was published by Pope Paul VI on 19 March 1969, in accordance with the directives of Vatican II.[17] *The Pastoral Constitution on the Church in the Modern World* devoted an entire chapter to the "Dignity of Marriage and Family Life."[18] It is clear from this chapter that Vatican II viewed the status of marriage as an urgent human problem and, therefore, wanted to support and encourage a renewed understanding of marriage in light of the church's teaching and tradition.

> The well-being of the individual person and of both human and Christian society is closely bound up with the healthy state of conjugal and family life. Hence Christians today are overjoyed, and so too are all who esteem conjugal and family life highly, to witness the various ways in which progress is being made in fostering those partnerships of love and in encouraging reverence for human life; there is progress too in services available to married people and

parents for fulfilling their lofty calling: even greater benefits are to be expected and efforts are being made to bring
them about.

However, this happy picture of the dignity of these partner-
ships is not reflected everywhere, but is overshadowed by
polygamy, the plague of divorce, so-called free love, and similar blemishes; furthermore, married love is too often dishon-
ored by selfishness, hedonism, and unlawful contraceptive
practices. Besides, the economic, social, psychological, and
civil climate of today has a severely disturbing effect on family
life. There are also the serious and alarming problems arising
in many parts of the world as a result of population expansion. On all of these counts an anguish of conscience is being
generated. And yet the strength and vigor of the institution of
marriage and family shines forth time and again: for despite
the hardships flowing from the profoundly changing conditions of society today, the true nature of marriage and of the
family is revealed in one way or another.

It is for these reasons that the Council intends to present
certain key points of the Church's teaching in a clearer light;
and it hopes to guide and encourage Christians and all men
who are trying to preserve and to foster the dignity and
supremely sacred value of the married state.[19]

It is clear from this passage that Vatican II recognized the variety
of problems facing married couples and set some ambitious goals
for assisting Christians in living the vocation of marriage within
the context of gospel values. Vatican II defined marriage as
authored and ordained by God, as an "intimate partnership of life
and love," "ordered to the procreation and education of the offspring."[20] Marriage and family life is the most common path to
holiness for Christians. Vatican II defined married love as a union
of the human and the divine which "leads the partners to a free
and mutual giving of self, experienced in tenderness and action."
The unity of marriage is found in the "equal personal dignity
which must be accorded to man and wife in mutual and unre-
served affection."[21] While recognizing that the procreation of children is only one result of marriage, Vatican II emphasized the
importance of family life and Christian education. But marriage

and family life is not simply the concern of married couples or of the church.

> The family is the place where different generations come together and help one another to grow wiser and harmonize the rights of individuals with other demands of social life; as such it constitutes the basis of society. Everyone, therefore, who exercises an influence in the community and in social groups should devote himself effectively to the welfare of marriage and the family. Civil authority should consider it a sacred duty to acknowledge the true nature of marriage and the family, to protect and foster them, to safeguard public morality and promote domestic prosperity. The rights of parents to procreate and educate children in the family must be safeguarded. There should also be welfare legislation and provision of various kinds made for the protection and assistance of those who unfortunately have been deprived of the benefits of family life.[22]

The Pastoral Constitution on the Church in the Modern World clearly attempts to call upon the entire world to assist married couples in fulfilling both their human and divine vocation.

The *Rite of Marriage* includes the following material: an introduction which articulates the importance and dignity of the sacrament of marriage; the rite for celebrating marriage during mass; the rite for celebrating marriage outside mass; the rite for celebrating marriage between a Catholic and an unbaptized person; and texts for use in the marriage rite and in the wedding mass, including scripture passages, prayers and blessings. In the introduction to the *Rite of Marriage,* encouragement is given to local conferences of bishops to adapt the rite to various cultures and marriage customs.[23]

The rite for celebrating marriage during mass is the usual way baptized Catholics celebrate the sacrament of marriage. During the entrance rite the priest greets the couple at the doors of the church and escorts them to the altar. During the liturgy of the word appropriate scripture passages are selected so that the homily can focus on marriage as a sacrament of the mystery of Christ and the church, the dignity of married love and the responsibilities of married people.

After the homily the actual rite of marriage is celebrated. The priest addresses the couple in the following words:

> My dear friends, you have come together in this church so that the Lord may seal and strengthen your love in the presence of the Church's minister and this community. Christ abundantly blesses this love. He has already consecrated you in baptism and now he enriches and strengthens you by a special sacrament so that you may assume the duties of marriage in mutual and lasting fidelity. And so, in the presence of the Church, I ask you to state your intentions.[24]

The priest then asks several questions of the couple to confirm that they are entering the marriage freely, that they promise to be faithful to one another for the rest of their lives, and that they will accept the possibility of children and the responsibility of bringing them up in the faith. This instruction and questioning reveal a theology of marriage that emphasizes the connection between baptism and marriage as a path to holiness, and the family as a domestic church.

The priest then invites the couple to declare their consent by exchanging their marriage vows in the presence of the assembled community. Several options are presented for this purpose. In the presence of the priest, two witnesses and the assembly, the couple joins hands and declares their consent:

> I, N., take you, N., to be my wife. I promise to be true to you in good times and in bad, in sickness and in health. I will love you and honor you all the days of my life.

> I, N., take you, N., to be my husband. I promise to be true to you in good times and in bad, in sickness and in health. I will love you and honor you all the days of my life.[25]

The priest then receives their consent:

> You have declared your consent before the Church. May the Lord in his goodness strengthen your consent and fill you both with his blessings. What God has joined, men must not divide.[26]

The priest then blesses the wedding rings and the couple exchanges them. The eucharist continues with the general intercessions, the preparation of the gifts and the liturgy of the eucharist.

After the Lord's Prayer, the priest gives the nuptial blessing, which beautifully articulates the church's hope and prayer that through marriage and family life the couple will be true to the commandments, faithful in marriage and living examples of Christian life. Eucharist continues as usual until the final blessing, which includes several options for blessing the bride and groom.

The rite for celebrating marriage outside mass and the rite for celebrating marriage between a Catholic and an unbaptized person are essentially the same as the rite just described, except that eucharist is not celebrated. These rites are used in several circumstances: a marriage between a Catholic and a baptized Christian; a marriage celebrated by a deacon, or other person delegated by the local conference of bishops, because no priest is available; or a marriage between a Catholic and an unbaptized person. Since the eucharist is a sign of the unity of the church, and since only Catholics can receive the eucharist, these rites demonstrate the church's sensitivity to the fact that the unity of the sacrament of marriage need not be jeopardized during the eucharist, in which the non-Catholic party cannot fully participate.

The revised *Rite of Marriage* celebrates a couple's communion with God and unity with the church. Through the sacrament of marriage, couples live their baptismal commitment to work for the spread of God's kingdom of justice, love and peace. In the sacrament of marriage couples promise fidelity to one another within the context of family life, and love of neighbor within the context of the church and the world.

Pastoral Challenges

Marriage is a sacrament of fidelity, communion, love and undivided affection. Those who enter into a Christian marriage express their faith in God, Jesus and the church. Christian marriage is the usual way Christians live out their baptismal vocation to be a living sign and witness of Christ to the world through their love and service of God and neighbor. But as the *Pastoral Constitution on the Church in the Modern World* indicates, these lofty ideals exist within a world that does not always support a "healthy state of conjugal and family life."[27]

The first challenge in celebrating the *Rite of Marriage* is for the church to accept responsibility for offering adequate and practical marriage preparation programs for couples intending to marry in the Catholic church. Some of the components of marriage preparation programs are a theology of marriage, which emphasizes scripture and the church's tradition; an overview of the *Rite of Marriage,* including the theology inherent in the liturgy of the word and the prayers and blessings; the moral dimension of marriage, including practical assistance in making moral decisions; marriage as ministry to the church and the world; human relationship, communication and conflict resolution skills; love, intimacy and human sexuality; children, parenting and passing on the faith to children; and such practical matters as managing a household, finances, careers, etc. Many good marriage preparation programs exist which help support and encourage couples in understanding their ministry as married couples. While the length and type of these programs vary from parish to parish, teams of married couples and priests are challenged to provide adequate and practical programs which enable couples to understand the duties and responsibilities of Christian marriage.

A second challenge in celebrating the *Rite of Marriage* is for parishes to enable couples to see the actual sacramental celebration of marriage, not as a private, family celebration, but as a public act of worship on the part of the church. It is the church which celebrates the sacrament of marriage, and as such, the sacramental celebration witnesses to the church's unity and the presence of Christ. As an act of worship, Christian marriage is oriented toward communion with God as well as communion with the whole church. Couples who come to the church for Christian marriage do not have to invent a ritual to celebrate their marriage. Rather, they celebrate with the community of faith a communal act of worship which relies on the church's rich tradition of scripture, prayers, blessings and ritual gestures to celebrate within the community of faith a life-long commitment of love and fidelity to one another and the whole world. Parish communities can assist couples in celebrating the *Rite of Marriage* by providing them with assistance in selecting the various options provided for in the rite and in making the parish's liturgical resources available to the couple—music ministry, lectors, extraordinary ministers of the eucharist, hospitality ministers, etc.

A third challenge in celebrating the *Rite of Marriage* is that of providing ongoing formation and adult education opportunities for married couples throughout the course of their marriage. The sacramental celebration of the marriage is only the beginning of a lifelong journey of conversion for Christians who choose to live the sacrament of marriage. As couples face the inevitable joys and sorrows of marriage and family life, and the economic, social, psychological and civil pressures of our time, parish communities can provide essential support and encouragement to families to continue to grow in their faith and in their ability to make a significant contribution to the building up of the kingdom of God. In this regard, the church can assist those in mixed marriages (a marriage between a Catholic and a baptized non-Catholic) and marriages with disparity of cult (a marriage between a Catholic and a non-baptized person). Newly married couples in these marriages will benefit greatly from experienced couples in learning how to share their faith while respecting religious diversity.

A fourth challenge in celebrating the *Rite of Marriage* is the church's ministry to marriages in crisis. It is a fact of life that married couples sometimes experience tremendous crises in their marriages. Pastoral ministers can help married couples negotiate some of these crises, especially by referring couples to competent psychological resources. In some cases, however, the only resolution to the crisis may be an annulment. This is a formal declaration by the church that a marriage was null and void from the beginning. The annulment does not mean that the marriage had no significance or meaning, or that the children of the marriage are illegitimate. There are three canonical reasons generally given for annulments. The first is a lack of canonical form.

The marriage of Catholics must take place in the presence of a bishop, priest or deacon and two witnesses. If any of these elements is missing, then the marriage is annulled. The second is a defect of human consent. Marriage is always a free decision of both partners. If this free consent is missing because of immaturity, force, fear or the lack of intention to enter into a permanent and exclusive union, then the marriage can be annulled. The third is an invalidating impediment. Some examples of impediments to marriage include: being underage, possessing a blood relationship that is too close, inability to have sexual intercourse, priestly ordination, or the existing bond of a prior marriage. In these cases the marriage can be annulled.[28] Pastoral ministers who devote themselves to ministering to marriages in crisis, and who lead couples through the process of annulment, must also provide assistance after the annulment so that the parties to the marriage can deal with the inevitable pain and suffering they have experienced. In cases where it is not possible to find adequate public reasons for an annulment, some Catholic couples seek a civil divorce. Some of these persons remarry outside the church. In these cases the church is committed to a caring and compassionate ministry to these persons and to continuing efforts to reconcile them to the church and to enable them to live the faith to the best of their ability.

Summary

Most Christians live out their baptismal commitment within the context of Christian marriage and family life. In Christian marriage, couples commit themselves to a life of equal and intimate partnership in abiding love, and form a kind of domestic church where faith is nurtured and where they continue to grow in discipleship, fidelity and love of neighbor. Marriage is a community of life and love which promotes the mutual love of husband and wife and is open to the possibility of children. As a sacrament, marriage provides the family with the means to grow in holiness, and provides the church with a living witness to the presence of Christ through the ministry of married couples to the church and the world. The sacramental celebration of marriage is the beginning of a lifelong journey. All of the church's efforts to promote, encourage and support Christians in their vocation of marriage contribute to a healthy state of conjugal and family life for the church and the world.

Questions for Reflection and Discussion

1. How is the sacrament of marriage rooted in Jesus' command to love one's neighbor?

2. How are husbands and wives signs to the world of the love and faithfulness of Christ?

3. Why did Vatican II pay so much attention to marriage?

4. How is the sacrament of marriage related to baptism?

5. Why does our church insist on a significant preparation for couples entering a marriage?

6. Why are some marriages annulled by the church?

10

Orders

*C*harlie came out of the house and onto the front porch carrying his huge glass of iced tea. His step was quicker than usual. Muriel thought she even heard him humming. He brushed by her quickly and then turned around and kissed her on the cheek.

"My, aren't we in a good mood tonight?" giggled Muriel as she fixed her glasses and repositioned her sweater.

"It has been a wonderful day, honey." Charlie, who was not usually effervescent about anything, threw himself into his favorite porch rocker and threw his feet up on the banister.

Muriel kept looking at him in disbelief. Her Charlie just wasn't taken to freely expressing himself, particularly this late in the evening. She sat up straight to look closely at him. "Have you been drinking?"

"No, just this iced tea." Charlie began to rock himself and to talk about their day.

"Who would have ever thought that a kid like that, who has been walking past this house all these years, would one day be a priest?" Charlie rocked himself a little faster.

Muriel began to talk about Jim. He was a nice boy from the neighborhood. He was always pleasant and respectful. The neighborhood was surprised when he decided to enter the seminary. Many thought he was too good-looking to be a priest. Others thought that he should have pursued a career in baseball. He had won every trophy available in high school. Muriel thought that he had made a great choice because of his many qualities. He was fundamentally a kind person.

Charlie began to talk about the ceremony that they had attended earlier that day. Charlie was really impressed with the number of priests that were there and how many of them were young. Muriel talked about how beautiful the music was and what a great experience it was to hear so many men singing. Both agreed that the ordination

145

was one of the most beautiful experiences that they had ever had in their parish church.

Muriel said that the moment that moved her the most was when Jim lay down on the floor and the congregation sang the litany of the saints. Muriel thought of the great stories that she knew of some of the saints. It was wonderful that holy men and women from every age were being invoked to come to that church and bless the young man who was the center of attention. Muriel choked up a bit as she told Charlie how she felt during that litany when the names of Jim's parents were sung. She was sure that there was a St. Stephen somewhere, and surely a St. Gertrude, but these were the names of Jim's parents who had died in a car accident years ago. Muriel was sure that Stephen and Gertrude were saints who were praying with the whole church at that time. It gave her comfort.

Charlie said that the proudest moment of the celebration for him was when the man who had married him and Muriel forty years ago went forward and laid his hands on Jim in silence. Charlie was surprised at how old his friend Father Bertain had become. Still, when he saw the old man lay his hands on Jim's head, he felt that some sort of wonderful power was being given to a new generation. Charlie stopped rocking and became very serious.

"I could feel it," he said. "I could feel the power of God in that church. It almost made me afraid."

"You are getting real sentimental in your old age, Charlie, and I am getting cold." Muriel began to tidy up the porch, which was her usual signal that her day was done.

Charlie stood up and threw the remainder of his iced tea on the lawn. "Wait a minute," he said as he got close to Muriel. "I don't know that I understand how someone becomes a priest, but that moment when they were all laying hands on him, I wanted to raise my hand too. I have known Jim all his life. His parents were my best friends. I supported him and prayed for him and I am very happy for him. I wanted to raise my hand with that bishop and all those priests and show Jim that he was a priest for all of us."

Muriel smiled warmly at Charlie. She kissed him and said, "You should have raised your hand. I did."

Origins

Almost every religion designates certain persons to serve the community in a variety of leadership positions. Most frequently these persons serve as mediators between the sacred and the religious community; sometimes these persons are considered sacred themselves. But these religious leaders also serve the community in a variety of other ways:

> ...preserving and interpreting the knowledge which is sacred to their tradition, writing it down, teaching it to others. And their authority in the area of religion often extends into other areas, enabling them to act as rulers and judges in matters which are not strictly religious but which are sacred to the society in which they live. Nevertheless, in all these ways priests and their equivalents—shamans, diviners, healers, sorcerers, witches, gurus, prophets, rabbis, imams, and so on—act as mediators of the sacred, persons through which the sacred can be experienced or better understood or properly lived.[1]

The history of religions teaches us that these "sacred persons" function in a variety of ways, either independently or in groups; they can be young or old, male or female; born into their role or designated by the community; serve permanently in this position or only for a time. In most cases, those who function as "sacred persons" are initiated into this role through some kind of public ceremony—a ritual of ordination, consecration or designation.

Within Christianity, through the sacrament of orders, bishops, priests and deacons are ordained to serve the community in a special and significant way. The *Catechism of the Catholic Church* explains that the sacrament of holy orders or orders enables the church to carry out through history the mission and ministry which Christ entrusted to the apostles, and it includes three degrees: episcopate (bishops); presbyterate (priests); and diaconate (deacons). In the ancient Roman world, the word *ordination* incorporated a person into an *order*, an established civic governing body. In the church, ordination is a religious, liturgical act which consecrates, blesses and sacramentalizes persons into the order of bishops, priests or deacons. Through the sacrament of orders men are designated and delegated by the Christian community, through the power of the Holy Spirit, to function as "sacred persons" within the community of faith. The essential sign of the sacrament of orders is the laying on of hands by a bishop and a prayer of consecration.[2]

Like all of the other sacraments, orders is rooted in the mission and ministry of Jesus Christ. As Vatican II teaches:

> In order to shepherd the People of God and to increase its numbers without cease, Christ the Lord set up in his Church a variety of offices which aim at the good of the whole body. The holders of office, who are invested with a sacred power, are, in fact, dedicated to promoting the interests of their brethren, so that all who belong to the People of God, and are consequently endowed with true Christian dignity, may, through their free and well-ordered efforts towards a common goal, attain to salvation.[3]

For Christians, the sacrament of orders is an integral and natural development of the ministry, passion, death, resurrection and ascension of Christ. Throughout its history, the church has patterned the sacrament of orders on the gospels:

> The Lord Jesus, having prayed at length to the Father, called to himself those whom he willed and appointed twelve to be with him, whom he might send to preach the kingdom of God (cf. Mk 3:13-19; Mt 10:1-42). These apostles (cf. Lk 6:13) he constituted in the form of a college or permanent assembly, at the head of which he placed Peter, chosen from amongst them (cf. Jn 21:15-17). He sent them first of all to the children of Israel and then to all peoples (cf. Rom 1:16), so that, sharing in his power, they might make all peoples his disciples and sanctify and govern them (cf. Mt 28:16-20; Mk 16:15; Lk 24:45-48; Jn 20:21-23) and thus spread the Church and, administering it under the guidance of the Lord, shepherd it all days until the end of the world (cf. Mt 28:20). They were fully confirmed in this mission on the day of Pentecost (cf. Acts 2:1-16) according to the promise of the Lord: "You shall receive power when the Holy Ghost descends upon you; and you shall be my witnesses both in Jerusalem and in all Judea and Samaria, and to the remotest

part of the earth" (Acts 1:8). By preaching everywhere the Gospel (cf. Mk 16:20), welcomed and received under the influence of the Holy Spirit by those who hear it, the apostles gather together the universal Church, which the Lord founded upon the apostles and built upon blessed Peter their leader, the chief cornerstone being Christ Jesus himself (cf. Apoc 21:14; Mt 16:18; Eph 2:20).[4]

In the Roman Catholic tradition, the sacrament of orders is not simply a way of preserving some kind of sociological cohesion or merely a matter of the community selecting persons to function in roles of religious leadership. Orders enables the church to continue the mission and ministry of Jesus, through the power of the Holy Spirit, until the end of time.

The sacrament of orders, like the other sacraments, is rooted in the mission and ministry of Jesus, and especially in his call to discipleship. As a Jew Jesus was very familiar with the Old Testament notion of priesthood. Jews believed that God chose one of the twelve tribes of Israel, Levi, and set it apart to mediate between God and the Jews and to offer gifts and sacrifices for sin.[5] The New Testament, however, views Jesus as the fulfillment of the priesthood in that Jesus accomplished once and for all the redemption and salvation of the whole world.[6] For Christians Christ is the one, unique priest and mediator between God and the people. Yet there are two distinct ways Christians participate in the priesthood of Jesus Christ:

> Though they differ essentially and not only in degree, the common priesthood of the faithful and the ministerial or hierarchical priesthood are none the less ordered one to another; each in its own proper way shares in the one priesthood of Christ. The ministerial priest, by the sacred power that he has, forms and rules the priestly people; in the person of Christ he effects the eucharistic sacrifice and offers it to God in the name of all the people. The faithful indeed, by virtue of their royal priesthood, participate in the offering of the Eucharist. They exercise that priesthood, too, by the reception of the sacraments, prayer and thanksgiving, the witness of a holy life, abnegation and active charity.[7]

Thus the baptized share in the one priesthood of Christ by living according to the Holy Spirit—a life of faith, hope and charity. Through baptism the baptized follow in the footsteps of the Lord Jesus Christ. The ordained share in the one priesthood of Christ by living according to the Holy Spirit—a ministerial priesthood which is rooted in the common priesthood of the baptized. Through ordination, bishops, priests and deacons, also following in the footsteps of the Lord Jesus Christ, lead the church through various ministries of service to the church.

Historical Developments

The history and evolution of the sacrament of orders in the church is a rich and multifaceted one.[8] We will sketch in broad strokes some of the essential developments in the church's history and understanding of ministry. To be a minister in the church is to serve the church. The word *ministry* has a variety of meanings and applications, and theologian Richard McBrien is helpful in making some necessary distinctions in the use of this word, especially as it is used in the church. McBrien defines ministry in four ways:

1. *General/universal ministry* is any service (which is the root meaning of the word *ministry*) rendered to another person or group of people who happen to be in need of that service. The call to ministry in this first sense is rooted in our common *humanity*. In other words, every human being is called to general/universal ministry. In this sense ministry has nothing intrinsically to do with religion. Examples of this ministry include taking care of a single parent's children, shopping for an elderly neighbor, demonstrating against nuclear weapons, or contributing to a fund for starving people.

2. *General/specific ministry* is any special service rendered by people specifically called to serve others in the so-called helping professions and other service occupations such as nursing, social work, and legal aid. Their ministry is rooted not only in their humanity but also in a particular

competence that is publicly certified or validated in one way or another, such as by licensing.

3. *Christian/universal ministry* is any general service rendered to others in *Christ and because of Christ.* The call to ministry in this third sense is rooted in our *baptism and confirmation.* Accordingly every member of the Church is called to ministry in this sense. And, in fact, when Christians perform the services in general/universal ministry, their actions are Christian/universal if performed out of explicitly Christian motives.

4. *Christian/specific ministry* is any general service rendered to others in Christ and because of Christ *in the name of the Church and for the sake of helping the Church fulfill its mission.* The call to ministry in this fourth and most specific sense is rooted in some form or act of *designation* by the Church itself. Thus it is sometimes called *designated ministry.* Relatively few members of the Church are called to ministry in this sense.[9]

The sacrament of orders is an example of *Christian/specific ministry.* Bishops, priests and deacons serve the church, and are designated by the church, to act in the name of the church and for the sake of helping the church fulfill its mission. There are, however, other examples of Christian/specific ministry: teachers, catechists, directors and coordinators of religious education, lectors, eucharistic ministers, hospitality ministers, etc.

After the death and resurrection of Jesus Christ, the New Testament tells us that a variety of ministries existed within the first Christian communities. Because of their close association with Jesus, the twelve disciples held a special place of honor and significance with the community. But the twelve selected others to assist them in ministry: elders (chosen because of their wisdom, age and experience); prophets (chosen because of their charismatic ability to speak on behalf of God and to challenge the community to work for justice); and teachers (chosen because of their ability to explain the scriptures). In these first Christian communities there were a variety of ministries, but all of them were in the service of fulfilling the church's mission, which was the mission of Christ, the proclamation of the king-dom of God.[10]

During the first and second centuries, the most enduring leader of the Christian community to emerge is the bishop. Functioning as a kind of president, overseer and guardian of the community, the bishop serves the Christian community, and is the sole leader of a large geographic area. Ignatius of Antioch and Clement of Rome are two examples of bishops who pro-vided a kind of stable leadership in the church as it faced rapid expansion and the threat of persecutions. The bishops were assisted in their ministry by deacons. The major transition which occurred during this period was the move from a charismatic and informal style of leadership to a more institutionalized and formal style of leadership.

During the third through the fifth centuries, the ministry of bishops, priests and deacons becomes firmly established. Given the rapidly growing numbers of Christians, and the inability of the bishops to be present for every eucharist and baptism, the bishops ordain presbyters (priests) to preside over local Christian communities or parishes. The priest's primary service to the community was to preside at eucharist, baptize, reconcile and teach the faith. The deacon's primary service to the community was to assist the bishop, especially in caring for the poor. The bishop's primary service to the community was to proclaim God's word, forgive sins, preside over the eucharist, and super-vise the work of the presbyters and deacons. Additionally, bish-ops functioned in a collegial fashion and worked together with their brother bishops to govern the universal church.[11]

From the sixth through the twelfth centuries, due in part to the widespread influence of the monarchy as a system of organi-zation, the sacrament of orders becomes a way to designate bish-ops, priests and deacons as men set apart from the people. In previous centuries, men were ordained to serve the church, espe-cially to celebrate the eucharist and to administer the other sacraments, and also to serve in some civil functions—collecting certain taxes and presiding as civil judges. Ordination cere-monies began to reflect this distinction between the ordained and the baptized.

The bishop was anointed with holy chrism, the crozier (staff) and ring were given, and then he was enthroned. The priest was ordained with an anointing of the hands, the giving of bread and wine, and a second laying on of hands in view of the absolution of sins. These developments reflected Germanic emblems of power, a "princely" power for bishops and a cultic power for priests.[12]

These changes reflect an important development in the sacrament of orders, especially the universal practice of celibacy in the twelfth century. Since the beginning of Christianity, celibacy as a way of life was an option, modeled on the fact that Jesus was celibate. However, it was not until the third century that some bishops and church councils began to require celibacy for clergy. By the twelfth century, due in large part to the reforms of Pope Gregory VII, celibacy was a universal practice in western Christianity.[13]

A monastic model of priesthood also emerged in the early Middle Ages, pushing the priesthood toward even more of a castelike existence within the Church. This movement reached its apex with the imposition of *celibacy* in the twelfth century as a universal requirement for priests of the Latin rite.[14]

The dramatic changes in the understanding of the role of bishops, priests and deacons during this period are due in large part to cultural influences.

Martin Luther's Reformation caused a serious split within Christianity—the so-called Protestant/Catholic division. Luther believed that there was only one priesthood of all believers—baptism. He rejected, therefore, the sacrament of orders, and saw no need for the ministry of bishop, priest and deacon. Luther believed that any specialized ministry that needed to be done should be delegated by the local community.

The *Council of Trent* rejected these views, declaring that the ordained priesthood, separate from and superior to the priesthood of all believers, is conferred through one of the seven sacraments, that the Mass is a true sacrifice, and that there is a true hierarchy in the Church consisting of bishops,

priests, and deacons and that these ministers do not depend
on the call of the community for their authority and powers.[15]

The teachings of the Council of Trent influenced the church
until the Second Vatican Council (1962–65). One of Trent's most
significant developments was the establishment of seminaries for
the education and training of priests. Seminaries ensured the
fact that future priests would be properly trained in scripture,
tradition, the celebration of the sacraments, and a lifestyle that
promoted a priestly spirituality which further distinguished the
ordained from the baptized.

Prior to and during Vatican II, the church attempted to
restore the sacrament of orders to its more original focus. This
restored and renewed understanding of orders is presented especially in the *Dogmatic Constitution on the Church,* which emphasizes the one priesthood of Christ expressed in two different
ways—the priesthood of baptism and the priesthood of ordination, which differ "in essence and not only in degree" (number
10). The bishops, successors to the apostles and united with the
bishop of Rome (the pope), function in a collegial fashion to
unite and govern the universal church (numbers 22 and 23).
Priests participate in the ministry of bishops and collaborate
with them in uniting and governing local parish communities.
Vatican II restored the diaconate, which had died out during the
sixteenth century, and allowed for the ordination of married
men to the diaconate to assist bishops and priests in their ministry and service to the church.

Theology and Celebration of the Rite

The revised rites for the ordination of deacons, priests and
bishops were published by Pope Paul VI on 18 June 1968.[16] Following the directives of Vatican II, these revised rites reflect the
general liturgical norms outlined by Vatican II, rely on the
ancient tradition of the church in ordination rituals, and articulate more clearly the ministry of deacons, priests and bishops.
The revised ritual includes the following: admission to candidacy
for ordination as deacons and priests; ordination of a deacon;

ordination of a priest; ordination of deacons and priests in the same celebration; ordination of a bishop; texts for use in ordinations; and an appendix which includes the blessing of pontifical insignia and the reception of the bishop in the cathedral church.

The rite for the ordination of a priest usually takes place on a Saturday or Sunday, in the cathedral or another large church. The eucharist begins in the usual way, with the candidate for ordination joining in the entrance procession. After the gospel, the bishop, wearing his miter, sits in his chair and the deacon calls the candidate forward. A priest designated by the bishop presents the candidate to the bishop, who inquires about his readiness for ordination. The priest responds:

> After inquiry among the people of Christ and upon recommendation of those concerned with his training, I testify that he has been found worthy.[17]

The bishop then responds:

> We rely on the help of the Lord God and our Savior Jesus Christ, and we choose this man, our brother, for priesthood in the presbyteral order.[18]

The assembled community then gives their assent to the ordination by responding, "Thanks be to God."

The bishop then gives the homily in which he explains to the assembly and the candidate the duties and responsibilities of the priest. A sample text of the homily is provided in the rite. It emphasizes the centrality of Christ and the participation of all of the baptized in the one priesthood of Christ, and the fact that Christ selected some of his followers to closely collaborate with him in the ministry of teaching, governing and sanctifying. The following sections of the sample homily clearly articulate the ministry of priest:

> My son, you are now to be advanced to the order of the presbyterate. You must apply your energies to the duty of teaching in the name of Christ, the chief Teacher. Share with all mankind the word of God you have received with joy. Meditate on the law of God, believe what you read,

teach what you believe, and put into practice what you
teach.

When you baptize, you will bring men and women into the
people of God. In the sacrament of penance, you will forgive
sins in the name of Christ and the Church. With holy oil you
will relieve and console the sick. You will celebrate the
liturgy and offer thanks and praise to God throughout the
day, praying not only for the people of God but for the
whole world. Remember that you are chosen from among
God's people and appointed to act for them in relation to
God. Do your part in the work of Christ the Priest with genuine joy and love, and attend to the concerns of Christ
before your own.[19]

This instruction to the candidate for ordination expresses in a
clear and beautiful way the church's understanding of the ministry of priesthood, a service to the church, modeled on the
example of Jesus Christ.

After the homily the bishop questions the candidate, who
publicly declares his resolve to faithfully fulfill the duties and
responsibilities of priesthood to the church and in collaboration
with the bishop. The bishop then invites the assembly to join in
prayer and in the litany of the saints.

Following the ancient tradition of the church, the ordination of the priest occurs through the silent laying on of hands by
the bishop, followed by the silent laying on of hands by all priests
present for the ordination, and the prayer of consecration:

Come to our help, Lord, holy Father, almighty and eternal
God; you are the source of every honor and dignity, of all
progress and stability. You watch over the growing family of
man by your gift of wisdom and your pattern of order.
When you had appointed high priests to rule your people,
you chose other men next to them in rank and dignity to be
with them and to help them in their task; and so there grew
up the ranks of priests and the offices of levites, established
by sacred rites.

In the desert you extended the spirit of Moses to seventy
wise men who helped him to rule the great company of his

people. You shared among the sons of Aaron the fullness of their father's power, to provide worthy priests in sufficient number for the increasing rites of sacrifice and worship. With the same loving care you gave companions to your Son's apostles to help in teaching the faith: they preached the Gospel to the whole world.

Lord, grant also to us such fellow workers, for we are weak and our need is greater.

Almighty Father, grant to this servant of yours the dignity of the priesthood. Renew within him the Spirit of holiness. As a co-worker with the order of bishops may he be faithful to the ministry that he receives from you, Lord God, and be to others a model of right conduct.

May he be faithful in working with the order of bishops, so that the words of the Gospel may reach the ends of the earth, and the family of nations, made one in Christ, may become God's one, holy people.

We ask this through our Lord Jesus Christ, your Son, who lives and reigns with you and the Holy Spirit, one God, for ever and ever. Amen.[20]

This prayer is followed by the investiture with the stole and chasuble and the anointing of the hands of the priest with the oil of chrism. The bishop then presents the priest with the gifts of bread and wine, saying:

Accept from the holy people of God the gifts to be offered to him. Know what you are doing, and imitate the mystery you celebrate: model your life on the mystery of the Lord's cross.[21]

The bishop then extends the sign of peace to the newly ordained and eucharist continues as usual.

The ordination of a deacon follows the same general pattern we have just described for the ordination of a priest, but with some obvious differences. In the homily to the candidates for the diaconate, the bishop outlines the unique duties of the deacon:

He will draw new strength from the gift of the Holy Spirit. He will help the bishop and his body of priests as a minister of the word, of the altar, and of charity. He will make himself a servant to all. As a minister of the altar he will proclaim the Gospel, prepare the sacrifice, and give the Lord's body and blood to the community of believers.

It will also be his duty, at the bishop's discretion, to bring God's word to believer and unbeliever alike, to preside over public prayer, to baptize, to assist at marriages and bless them, to give viaticum to the dying, and to lead the rites of burial. Once he is consecrated by the laying on of hands that comes to us from the apostles and is bound more closely to the altar, he will perform works of charity in the name of the bishop or the pastor. From the way he goes about these duties, may you recognize him as a disciple of Jesus, who came to serve, not to be served.[22]

The candidate for the diaconate is ordained through the silent laying on of hands of the bishop alone and a prayer of consecration. This is followed by investiture with the stole and dalmatic and the presentation of the *Book of the Gospels*. The rite for the ordination of a deacon clearly emphasizes the ministry of the deacon in the church: assisting the bishops and priests as a minister of the word, engaging in works of charity, and presiding at baptisms, marriages, viaticum to the dying and Christian burial.

The ordination of a bishop also follows this same general pattern, but with some important differences. At least two bishops are required for the ordination of a bishop, following the ancient custom of the church. During the imposition of hands, all of the bishops present lay hands in silence on the bishop-elect. The homily and the prayer of consecration clearly articulate the ministry of the bishop in the church:

You, dear brother, have been chosen by the Lord. Remember that you are chosen from among men and appointed to act for men and women in relation to God. The title of bishop is one not of honor but of function, and therefore a bishop should strive to serve rather than to rule. Such is the counsel of the Master: the greater should behave as if he were the least, and the leader as if he were the one who serves.[23]

The homily and prayer of consecration emphasize the bishop's responsibility to serve the church as a faithful overseer and guardian, working in collaboration with all bishops in the ministry of teaching, governing and sanctifying. The bishop-elect is instructed to pay special attention to proclaiming the word of God and compassionately caring for all those entrusted to his care.

The rite for the ordination of deacons, priests and bishops clearly articulates the ancient tradition of the church in the sacrament of orders. Through this sacrament the church continues the mission and ministry of Christ, through the power of the Holy Spirit.

Pastoral Challenges

The first challenge in celebrating the sacrament of orders is really a challenge for the entire church. This sacrament is essential and necessary so that all of the baptized can participate in the ministry of Christ. Those ordained as deacons, priests and bishops exercise a ministry of leadership, enabling the church, a universal community of faith consisting of millions of people, to follow in the footsteps of Jesus Christ. The sacrament of orders provides for a "sense of order" in the church, but more importantly, it provides for a continuity of faith among the believers in every land and nation. The sacrament of orders challenges the ordained and the baptized to keep Christ at the center of the church and the world. Christ's ministry of service and proclamation of the word of God and the kingdom of God is precisely the challenge of all who profess faith through baptism, confirmation and eucharist.

A second challenge in celebrating the sacrament of orders is its emphasis on ministry and service to the community of faith, and indeed, to all the world. Deacons, priests and bishops are ordained to serve the needs of the church, but also to move the entire church to serve the needs of the world. Jesus Christ is the model for this. Matthew's parable of the judgment of the nations (25:31–46), and the entire ministry of Jesus, challenges the church, and especially the ordained, to identify and respond to the variety of needs evident in the world of our own day. The sacramental ministry of the ordained challenges all of the baptized to participate in the one priesthood of Christ, especially his ministry of charity and service. The challenge of the sacrament of orders is to bring the gospel of Jesus Christ, and its ethical and moral demands, to those so desperately in need.

A third challenge in celebrating the sacrament of orders is to recruit and train men for ordained ministry in the church. Many young people are interested in careers in the helping professions in general, and in responding to their baptismal commitment to service of the poor. This is a very encouraging sign for the future of the church. Following the example of Jesus, the church needs to be bold in its efforts to invite qualified young men to seriously consider ministry in the church, especially through ordination as deacons and priests. The sacrament of orders challenges the baptized and the ordained to nurture the gift of faith within family life and parish community. Additionally, seminaries are challenged to offer appropriate training for those who desire ordination. The challenge here is for adequate academic programs that provide sound theological expertise, and pastoral training that provides a variety of hands-on experiences in serving the various needs of the church.

A fourth challenge in the sacrament of orders is to provide ongoing education, formation and support to the ordained. Like many of the other sacraments, the rite of ordination of deacons, priests and bishops is only the beginning of a lifelong conversion to the Lord Jesus Christ. The ordained, much like persons in the other helping professions, need and require opportunities to deepen and strengthen their own commitment to and understanding of their ministry. The sacrament of orders challenges the ordained to nurture their own faith through prayer and retreat programs, through theological and ministerial update programs, and through healthy and supportive relationships with people.

Summary

For nearly two thousand years, through the sacrament of orders, the church has ordained men to a ministry of service for the sake of helping the church fulfill its mission. Bishops, priests and deacons, responding to the call of God and the invitation of the church, have spread the gospel of Jesus Christ to the ends of the earth. The ordained, sensitive to the variety of needs of people throughout history, have responded in charismatic and institutionalized ways to Christ's command to spread the good news to all the world. Throughout history the sacrament of orders has enabled the word of God to be preached, the sacraments to be celebrated, and works of charity embraced.

Questions for Reflection and Discussion

1. In what way do bishops, priests and deacons function as "sacred persons" within the community of faith?

2. How is the priesthood of all the baptized different from the priesthood conferred in holy orders?

3. How do priests share in the ministry of bishops?

4. What is the emphasis in the ordination of deacons?

5. How is the laying on of hands similar and different in the ordination of bishops, priests and deacons?

11

The Ritual Life
of the Parish

*M*arie *always liked this day. Whenever one of her grandchildren turned five she would take them to church with her and give them the grand tour. She had done it six times before, but today she was taking Elizabeth. Marie worked very hard in making sure that no one knew that Elizabeth was her favorite. Everybody knew it anyway.*

Marie picked up Elizabeth about a half hour before mass. Elizabeth loved being with her grandmother and was very excited that this day would be her birthday present. Marie took Elizabeth by the hand and warned her that she needed to be very good because they were going to visit God's house.

Elizabeth had been to the church before. She knew it was God's house. It was a really big building, big enough for God. But she was sure that she had never seen God in his house.

Marie took the little girl to the holy water fount. She told her that today was the day she would learn how to make the sign of the cross. Elizabeth liked dipping her hand in the water and splashing it some.

"You can't do that," Marie said as she firmly grabbed the little girl's hand. "This is special water. It reminds you of your baptism."

"When was that, Grandma?" Elizabeth seemed to listen with her eyes.

"When you were born we all loved you very much. Your Mom and Dad brought you to this church. It was the first time you were ever out of your house. They poured water on your head to make sure that there were no sins on you. They baptized you in the name of the Father, the Son and the Holy Spirit. That's why we take this water and touch our head, and then our heart, and then the left shoulder and right shoulder. When you are baptized you become part of Jesus' family."

Elizabeth smiled and tried to make the sign of the cross. She got mixed up a couple of times and wasn't sure of when to go left or right. Marie was pretty sure that she had enough water on her so she moved into the church.

Marie showed Elizabeth where she was baptized. Then she showed her the tabernacle. Again she made the sign of the cross. Elizabeth loved all the candles that were glowing all over the church. Marie explained how people light a candle so that their prayers keep on going even after they go home.

Elizabeth tried the sign of the cross again. "You're getting it," Marie said, and she hugged her grandchild.

Marie then took the little girl around the church and showed her where her parents stood when they got married. She also told her about the statues and how Catholics remember the saints. She showed her the stations of the cross and the reconciliation room. Elizabeth was surprised that there were so many things to do in God's house.

Marie took Elizabeth to the statue of the Blessed Virgin Mary. She told the girl to kneel down and they would say a prayer that Mary would watch over her and bless her.

Elizabeth bowed her head and became very serious. Finally she said, "Grandma, if this is God's house how come I can't see him?"

Marie hugged the child even tighter. "Elizabeth, just always remember that God loves you very much. If you keep growing up as beautiful as you are, you will see God all over this place."

Elizabeth shook her head. That made sense. She tried one more time to make the sign of the cross and then she really brightened up. "Grandma, look!" she said. "The Holy Spirit is on my shoulder."

Introduction

In addition to the sacraments, which are the primary way the church gives praise and thanks to God, there are many other forms of prayer and worship, many other forms of piety and devotion, which fill the days and seasons of a Christian's life. These additional forms of prayer and worship are called *sacramentals:*

> Sacramentals are instituted for the sanctification of certain ministries of the Church, certain states of life, a great variety of circumstances in Christian life, and the use of many things

helpful to man. In accordance with the bishops' decisions, they can also respond to the needs, culture, and special history of the Christian people of a particular region or time. They always include a prayer, often accompanied by a specific sign, such as the laying on of hands, the sign of the cross, or the sprinkling of holy water (which recalls Baptism).[1]

These special forms of prayer and devotion emerged, and continue to emerge, in the life of the Christian community to enable Christians to celebrate the holiness of daily living, the sacredness of special events, places, objects and persons, and ultimately to enable Christians to treasure the values and wisdom contained in the gospels and the tradition of the church.[2]

In its reform of the liturgical life of the church, Vatican II emphasized the important role sacramentals play in the spiritual life of Christians:

> Holy Mother Church has, moreover, instituted sacramentals. These are sacred signs which bear a resemblance to the sacraments. They signify effects, particularly of a spiritual nature, which are obtained through the Church's intercession. By them men are disposed to receive the chief effect of the sacraments, and various occasions in life are rendered holy.
>
> Thus, for well-disposed members of the faithful the liturgy of the sacraments and sacramentals sanctifies almost every event of their lives with the divine grace which flows from the paschal mystery of the Passion, Death and Resurrection of Christ. From this source all sacraments and sacramentals draw their power. There is scarcely any proper use of material things which cannot thus be directed toward the sanctification of men and the praise of God.[3]

Sacramentals enable Christians to nourish their spirituality— their existential experience of life, centered on Jesus Christ and directed by the power of God's Holy Spirit.

In this chapter we will consider several ways Christians ritualize the sacredness of daily living through worship and prayer: the *Order of Christian Funerals,* the liturgy of the hours, holy communion and worship of the eucharist outside mass, *The Book of Blessings* and various devotions.

The Order of Christian Funerals

The death of loved ones is a difficult and challenging experience for Christians; however, death is a passage from this life to life forever with God in the kingdom. In the creed Christians pray for the resurrection of the dead and the life of the world to come. Through baptism, confirmation and eucharist Christians are initiated into the church; the *Order of Christian Funerals* marks the end of earthly life and initiation into eternal life. For the deceased, death is the end. The celebration of a Christian funeral, therefore, does nothing for the deceased, but rather unites the living in a spirit of communion and fellowship with those who have died and expresses the faith of the church in the resurrection of the just.

The Congregation for Divine Worship approved the revised *Order of Christian Funerals* on 14 November 1985, and it was published by the National Conference of Catholic Bishops on 15 August 1989.[4] The celebration of Christian funerals includes three stages of prayer and worship: in the home or funeral parlor, including prayers after death, gathering in the presence of the body, and the vigil for the deceased with reception at the church; the funeral liturgy, including a funeral mass and a funeral liturgy outside mass; and the rite of committal, celebrated at the grave, tomb, or crematorium.[5] The *Order of Christian Funerals* provides a rich variety of prayers designed to enhance the church's celebration of the death of Christians—bishops, priests, deacons, religious, married people, infants, children, young adults, elderly people—who die in a variety of circumstances—after a long illness, suddenly, accidentally, violently or as a result of suicide.[6]

After death, it is usually the custom to wake the deceased in a funeral home, and sometimes in the family home or the parish church. The vigil for the deceased is the church's primary act of worship prior to the funeral mass. The purpose of this time of vigil and prayer is beautifully expressed in the *Order of Christian Funerals*:

> At the vigil the Christian community keeps watch with the family in prayer to the God of mercy and finds strength in

Christ's presence. It is the first occasion among the funeral
rites for the solemn reading of the word of God. In this time
of loss the family and community turn to God's word as the
source of faith and hope, as light and life in the face of darkness and death. Consoled by the redeeming word of God
and by the abiding presence of Christ and his Spirit, the
assembly at the vigil calls upon the Father of mercy to
receive the deceased into the kingdom of light and peace.[7]

Several options for the vigil for the deceased are provided,
which generally include the following: a greeting and opening
prayer; a liturgy of the word and homily; prayers of intercession
and the Lord's Prayer; and a concluding prayer and blessing. As
family, friends and other members of the Christian community
gather for the vigil for the deceased, they express through worship and prayer their desire to find strength and hope in the
word of God and in the consolation of one another.

At the funeral liturgy, usually celebrated within the context
of eucharist, family, friends and other members of the parish
community gather with a specific purpose in mind:

...to give praise and thanks to God for Christ's victory over
sin and death, to commend the deceased to God's tender
mercy and compassion, and to seek strength in the proclamation of the paschal mystery. Through the Holy Spirit the
community is joined together in faith as one Body in Christ
to reaffirm in sign and symbol, word and gesture that each
believer through baptism shares in Christ's death and resurrection and can look to the day when all the elect will be
raised up and united in the kingdom of light and peace.[8]

The funeral eucharist is much like any other celebration of the
eucharist, except for the following. During the introductory rites
the family of the deceased brings the body to the door of the
church where the priest greets the family and sprinkles the cof-
fin with holy water and covers it with the pall, a white cloth
which, together with the holy water, recalls baptism. During the
liturgy of the word, scripture passages are selected which focus
on the paschal mystery and the church's belief in death and the
resurrection of the just. In place of the customary concluding

rites, a final prayer of commendation and procession to the place of burial takes place.

The final act of worship takes place when Christians gather to finally bury the dead, usually at the grave, tomb, or crematorium. The rite of committal with final commendation is a simple prayer service which includes an invitation to prayer, a brief scripture reading, a prayer over the place of committal, words of committal, the intercessions and the Lord's Prayer, and a concluding prayer and blessing.

> In committing the body to its resting place, the community expresses the hope that, with all those who have gone before marked with the sign of faith, the deceased awaits the glory of the resurrection. The rite of committal is an expression of the communion that exists between the Church on earth and the Church in heaven: the deceased passes with the farewell prayers of the community of believers into the welcoming company of those who need faith no longer but see God face to face.[9]

The church's worship and prayer at the time of death enable Christians to profess faith in Jesus Christ, give witness to their hope in the resurrection, and experience the hope and consolation of family, friends and the entire Christian community.

The Liturgy of the Hours

The liturgy of the hours, formerly known as the divine office, is probably not very familiar to most Christians. However, the Second Vatican Council ordered a restoration of this ancient practice of prayer in the church and urged that especially morning prayer and evening prayer begin to be celebrated in parishes, by all of the baptized.[10] Gradually, many parish communities are learning to worship with the liturgy of the hours because it "bridges the gap between our daily living and our religious experience."[11]

The gospels tell us that Jesus prayed both privately (Mk 7:34; Lk 3:21–22; 6:12; 9:28–30) and communally (Lk 4:16). The New Testament tells us that the early Christians followed Jesus' custom and gathered regularly for prayer (Acts 2:46; 13:14–15;

1 Thes 1:2). During the third and fourth centuries, the liturgy of the hours began to develop as a structured and formal way for Christians to pray in their local churches. The times for this prayer expanded to include: morning prayer, midday prayer, evening prayer, night prayer, and nighttime vigil prayer. History indicates that the practice of the liturgy of the hours varied, but by the time of the reformation and the Council of Trent it had become almost exclusively the required daily prayer of clerics and monastics.[12]

Morning prayer and evening prayer are the two most common ways Christians use the liturgy of the hours. These prayers usually consist of the following: an invitation to prayer and hymn; several psalms; a scripture reading with a responsorial psalm and homily; the gospel canticle (Benedictus for morning prayer and Magnificat for evening prayer); intercessions and the Lord's Prayer; concluding prayer, blessing and dismissal. Morning and evening prayer are designed to be celebrated as communal worship and can be presided over by a priest, deacon or lay person. As communal acts of worship, they can include music and singing. *Christian Prayer: The Liturgy of the Hours* is the official, one-volume book of the church's revised rites for this prayer, though many other resources are available for individuals and parish communities.[13]

Many Christians today are searching for ways to develop a genuine and regular way to pray. The liturgy of the hours, especially morning and evening prayer, offers Christians the possibility of doing that, either individually or communally, so that they can unite their daily joys and sufferings to those of Christ, who redeemed the world through his own constant praise, thanksgiving and petition to God.

Holy Communion and Worship of the Eucharist Outside Mass

Prior to Vatican II, benediction, the annual forty hours, devotion, and prayer before the reserved blessed sacrament (tabernacle) were very popular among Catholics. A variety of historical circumstances and theological debates made these customs a regular part of Catholic worship and prayer. Adoration and worship of the eucharist outside of mass is a tradition that can be traced back to Justin Martyr in the second century; however, it really flourished in the church from the thirteenth to the mid-twentieth century. Throughout the history of the development of these eucharistic devotions, an emphasis on the eucharist as the central act of the church's worship was always kept in mind, as was the responsibility of Christians to unite themselves frequently in the active celebration of the eucharist.[14]

Eucharistic devotions, such as those mentioned above, have declined since the liturgical reforms of Vatican II. The chief reason for this is the enhanced understanding of eucharist which Vatican II articulated for the church. Vatican II urged active and full celebration of the eucharist in the language of the people, and set in motion reforms which enable the baptized to recognize the many modes of Christ's presence in the assembly—the word of God, the bread and wine, and the dismissal of the assembly to be the body and blood of Christ in the world.

The National Conference of Catholic Bishops published the *Order for the Solemn Exposition of the Holy Eucharist* in 1992, based on liturgical reforms inaugurated by Vatican II and the Congregation for Divine Worship.[15] The essential link between eucharist and adoration of the eucharist outside mass is articulated in the following way:

> The solemn exposition of the holy eucharist offers the opportunity to the people of God for prayerful reflection on their call to a deeper devotion to the holy eucharist and a more faithful living of the Christian life. It provides them with an opportunity to become more aware of Christ's presence with his people and invites them to a spiritual communion with him.
>
> Prayer before Christ the Lord sacramentally present [in the eucharist] extends the union with Christ that the faithful have reached in communion. It renews the covenant that in turn moves them to maintain by the way they live what they have received through faith and the sacrament. They should strive to lead their whole lives in the strength of this heavenly food, as sharers in the death and resurrection of the Lord. All should be eager to do good works and to please

God, so that they may seek to imbue the world with the Christian spirit and, in all things, even in the midst of human affairs, to become witnesses of Christ.[16]

Worship of the eucharist outside mass is not a substitute for Sunday eucharist, but rather a means for extending the presence of Christ, through witness and active service of God and neighbor, to all areas of life.

The *Order for the Solemn Exposition of the Holy Eucharist* provides rituals for benediction, the annual forty hours, devotion, and the liturgy of the hours during a period of exposition. The prayer used to conclude all of these rituals expresses the theology and understanding of worship of the eucharist outside mass:

> Lord Jesus Christ, you gave us the eucharist as the memorial of your suffering and death. May our worship of this sacrament of your body and blood help us to experience the salvation you won for us and the peace of the kingdom where you live with the Father and the Holy Spirit, one God, for ever and ever. Amen.[17]

Through music and singing, the word of God and homily, intercessions and adoration, Christians renew their commitment to live the paschal mystery through all of their efforts to bring the body and blood of Christ to a spiritually hungry world.

The Book of Blessings

One of the great treasures in Vatican II's reform of the liturgy is *The Book of Blessings*. The official Latin edition was published by the Congregation for Divine Worship in 1984, and the National Conference of Catholic Bishops published the English edition on 19 March 1989. The English edition contains additional blessings and prayers composed for use in the United States.[18] The general introduction to *The Book of Blessings* explores the rich history and spiritual benefits of celebrating blessings in the life of a Christian.

A blessing prayer does not *make* some*thing* or some*one* holy. Blessing prayers express praise and thanks to God for the sacredness of all things and all peoples, and thus enable Christians to recognize God, Jesus Christ and the Holy Spirit as the origin and goal of life.

> The source from whom every good gift comes is God, who is above all, blessed for ever. He who is all good has made all things good, so that he might fill his creatures with blessings and even after the Fall he has continued his blessings as a sign of his merciful love.
>
> Christ, the Father's supreme blessing upon us, is portrayed in the gospel as blessing those he encountered, especially the children, and as offering to his Father prayers of blessing. Glorified by the Father, after his ascension Christ sent the gift of his Spirit upon the brothers and sisters he had gained at the cost of his blood. The power of the Spirit would enable them to offer the Father always and everywhere praise, adoration, and thanksgiving and, through the works of charity, to be numbered among the blessed in the Father's kingdom.[19]

Blessing prayers, therefore, enable Christians to give praise, adoration, and thanksgiving to God, modeled on the example of Jesus Christ, and through the power of the Holy Spirit, to engage in works of charity to bring God's presence and action to all the world.

> Whether God blessed the people himself or through the ministry of those who acted in his name, his blessing was always a promise of divine help, a proclamation of his favor, a reassurance of his faithfulness to the covenant he had made with his people. When, in turn, others uttered blessings, they were offering praise to the one whose goodness and mercy they were proclaiming.
>
> Blessings therefore refer first and foremost to God, whose majesty and goodness they extol, and, since they indicate the communication of God's favor, they also involve human beings, whom he governs and in his providence protects. Further, blessings apply to other created things through which, in their abundance and variety, God blesses human beings.[20]

Through blessing prayers Christians celebrate the goodness of all creation and the ever-present mystery of God.

The typical structure for a blessing prayer is rather simple: an introduction, which includes recalling the presence of God, Jesus and the Holy Spirit, and a brief instruction on the purpose of the blessing prayer; a proclamation of God's word, which may include a responsorial psalm, "to ensure that the blessing is a genuine sacred sign, deriving its meaning and effectiveness from God's word"[21]; a blessing prayer and ritual gesture, which may include prayers of intercession; and a concluding prayer and dismissal. The ritual gestures which are often included in blessing prayers are the outstretching, raising or joining of the hands; the laying on of hands; the sign of the cross; sprinkling with holy water; the lighting of candles; the use of incense, etc.[22]

The general introduction to *The Book of Blessings* indicates that the ministry of blessing belongs to all of the baptized. However, when blessing prayers are celebrated by the entire diocesan community, it is the place of the bishop to preside. When blessing prayers are celebrated by a parish community, the pastor or another priest presides. Other blessings may be celebrated by a deacon and many of the blessing prayers may be celebrated by the baptized.[23]

Part one of *The Book of Blessings* contains "Blessings Directly Pertaining to Persons." Blessings prayers are included for families, married couples, children, birthdays, the elderly, the sick, missionaries, catechists, students, teachers, pilgrims, travelers, etc. Part two contains "Blessings Related to Buildings and to Various Forms of Human Activity." Included here are blessings for homes, seminaries, schools, hospitals, various means of transportation, tools, animals, farms, meals, etc. Part three contains "Blessings of Objects that Are Designed or Erected for Use in Churches," including blessings for a baptistry, tabernacle, ambo, presidential chair, statues, holy water, stations of the cross, etc. Part four contains "Blessings of Articles Meant to Foster the Devotion of the Christian People"—religious articles, rosaries, scapulars, etc. Part five contains "Blessings Related to Feasts and Seasons." These blessings are generally related to the liturgical year and can be celebrated by parish communities or by families.

Blessings prayers in this section include the following: the blessing of an Advent wreath, Christmas manger and Christmas tree; the blessing of throats on the feast of St. Blase; the blessing and distribution of ashes on Ash Wednesday; the blessing of St. Joseph's table; the blessing of food for Thanksgiving Day; and a Mother's Day and Father's Day blessing. Part six contains "Blessings for Various Needs and Occasions," including the blessing of those engaged in pastoral service, lectors, altar servers, extraordinary ministers, parish councils, etc.

The Book of Blessings is a practical, convenient and inspirational way for Christians to give adoration, praise and thanksgiving to God for persons and things, indeed, for all of creation. Blessings prayers enable Christians to walk in the footsteps of Jesus Christ and to see all of life as a blessing from God.

Devotions

Devotions are unique features of Catholic life and worship. Devotions, either in the form of private or communal prayer, enable Catholics to nurture their faith and to engage their emotions as they strive to live the Christian life. Devotions are popular religious exercises (prayers, methods of meditation, rituals, gestures) which have grown up in the church in every culture and nation. Popular religious devotions include the rosary, the stations of the cross, novenas (nine consecutive days of prayer) and devotion to particular saints—Joseph, Anthony, Christopher, Therese of Lisieux, Mary, Catherine of Siena, etc. This tradition of Christian prayer and devotion is testimony to the fact that from the Acts of the Apostles to the present, Christians have treasured in their hearts a "profound grasp of the spiritual realities they experience" (Cf. *DV* 8).[24]

Popular religious devotions like those mentioned above enable Christians to focus their minds and hearts on the essentials of Christian faith. By praying the rosary and the stations of the cross, by celebrating novenas and praying to saints, Christians cultivate the mind and heart of Jesus Christ and practice the theological virtues (faith, hope and charity) and the cardinal or moral virtues (justice, fortitude, temperance and prudence).

Devotions are not a substitute for the sacraments and the word of God, but rather a necessary complement to the practice of living the Christian life.

The community of the saints and the various prayers and devotions that have grown up in the church serve to give Christians real life examples of what it means to be Christian in the world. Christians do not worship the saints. Christians do not substitute praying to the saints for praying to God, Jesus and the Holy Spirit.

> There exists a bond of confident intimacy *(communio)* between the saints and those on earth which enriches and deepens the relationship with Christ and with God. The theology of the veneration of the saints does not attempt to supplant the saving power of God by the saints. Imitation and invocation does not detract from the prerogatives of Christ, but serves to glorify his redemption. By extension of the theology of incarnation and redemption, invocation of the saints implies no essential addition to Christ's mediation but rather a realization of its potentialities and a subordinate cooperation of his members applying the fruits of his redemption. Through participation in the life of the Godhead, the saints continue to live some degree of divine life and as sharers in this divine life, they beseech God on our behalf.[25]

Most of the saints took a piece of the gospel and held it up for all to see. Some focused on service of the poor, others on justice, care of the sick and dying, Christian education, witnessing to the faith. In every case their devotion to part of the gospel of Jesus Christ enabled and inspired others to follow in the footsteps of Christ. The saints are objects of devotion and veneration precisely because they are brilliant lights leading the way to God in a world filled with so much darkness and confusion.

Conclusion

Ritualizing the sacredness of daily living through worship and prayer, Christians sacramentalize the whole of life and all of creation. In celebrating the resurrection of the dead and the life

of the world to come, in praying throughout the days and seasons of life, in celebrating the abiding presence of Christ, and in
worshiping with a variety of devotions and prayers, Christians
follow Paul's injunction:

> Rejoice always. Pray without ceasing. In all circumstances
> give thanks, for this is the will of God for you in Christ Jesus.
> Do not quench the Spirit. Do not despise prophetic utter-
> ances. Test everything; retain what is good. Refrain from
> every kind of evil.[26]

The ritual life of the parish nourishes Christians in their faithful
and spirit-filled journey of conversion to the Lord Jesus Christ.

Questions for Reflection and Discussion

1. What role do sacramentals play in the life of the community of
   faith?

2. What is the purpose of a funeral liturgy?

3. How does the liturgy of the hours give Christians a regular way of
   praying?

4. How is the worship of the eucharist outside of mass related to
   eucharist in mass?

5. Who does the ministry of blessing belong to in the church?

6. How do devotions focus the attention of Christians on the essential
   elements of Christian life?

Conclusion

*A*n *ancient rabbi once asked his disciples, "When is it light enough to see?" "I know," one answered. "It is light enough to see when I can distinguish an oak from a maple." "No," said the rabbi. "I know," a second volunteered. "It is light enough to see when I can tell a horse from a cow." "That is not correct either," noted the rabbi. There being no other attempts at an answer, the rabbi stated, "It is light enough to see when I can look a person in the face and recognize a brother or sister."[1]*

Jesus must have surely understood this ancient rabbinic insight—dawn comes into our lives when we can recognize all others as our sisters and brothers. Jesus Christ is the light of the world, a light which dispels the darkness, though many people still cling to the darkness. Luke's gospel, more than any other, tells us some of the stories of Jesus coming to faith within the context of family life. When the angel Gabriel announced to Mary that it was through the power of the Holy Spirit that she would give birth to Jesus, Mary was frightened. Gabriel reassured her, and Mary gave her unqualified *yes* to God. Mary then set out to visit her cousin, Elizabeth, who was about to give birth to John the Baptist. During the course of their visit, Mary expressed her faith in God and her gratefulness for the wonderful things God had done for her. Mary gave thanks that God is merciful. Mary understood that we are all brothers and sisters to one another, for God has raised up the lowly and fed the hungry—rulers are dethroned and the rich lose all they have. As Jesus began his public ministry, he was invited to read from the scriptures in his hometown synagogue. Jesus read the passage from Isaiah and identified his own mission with the text—a mission to the poor, the captives, the blind and the oppressed. And later on, in his sermon on the plain, Jesus called blessed those who were poor, hungry, sorrowful and persecuted. "But to you who hear I say, love your enemies, do good to those who hate you, bless those who curse you, pray for those who mistreat you."[2] Mary and Joseph recognized the truth of their faith in God, and passed on this faith to Jesus, who is for all Christians the light of the world.

The Christian sacraments and sacramentals initiate us into the life of faith, and throughout the course of our lives continue to nourish and sustain us in our journey of conversion to the Lord Jesus Christ. The ultimate test of our Christian faith is our ability to follow in the footsteps of Jesus Christ and to witness to the fact that all of us are sisters and brothers to one another.

The Christian sacraments and sacramentals are rooted in our human experience, modeled on the mission and ministry of Jesus Christ and the tradition of the church, and nourished by our experience of them as we challenge one another to celebrate them well with the community of faith and live them well in our homes, neighborhoods, schools, workplaces, and indeed, throughout all the world. The liturgical renewal inaugurated by the Second Vatican Council calls us to a full, conscious and active participation in the sacramental life of the church. Christians do not simply belong to the church, they are the church. Vatican II describes Christians as the people of God, a pilgrim people, a people on a lifelong journey of conversion.

> We journey on, attentive to the Lord who calls us into the desert to renew us and fashion us as his own, who guides us by his providential care, who sustains us along the journey, and who leads us home from our exiles. The Church can never settle down and become comfortable with what is but must journey ever on, attentive to the call of the Lord to serve him and his kingdom.
>
> In this present time, we are being called to trust in the providence of God and to allow him to purify us and renew us, to shape and mold us into what he wants us to be. This demands a spirituality of trusting, of letting go, of allowing one's vision to be sharpened anew, a spirituality in which the word and life are in constant dialogue.[3]

As the people of God, the church, through its celebration of the sacraments and the sacramentals, proclaims in word and in action the ongoing revelation of Jesus Christ. Through word and action the gospel of Jesus Christ is proclaimed to all the world as Christians engage themselves in the mission and ministry of Christ.

The sacraments and sacramentals of the church have their foundation in the preaching and teaching ministry of Jesus Christ. Relying on tangible, material reality, and as rituals, gestures and symbols which the church has designated to express its own reality, the sacraments and sacramentals celebrate the saving activity of God within the community of faith, which is always involved in both initial and ongoing conversion to the values of Jesus Christ.

Notes

Introduction

1. Elie Wiesel, *The Forgotten* (New York: Summit Books, 1992), 11–12.
2. *Catechism of the Catholic Church* for the United States of America (Washington, D.C.: United States Catholic Conference Inc., Libreria Editrice Vaticana, 1994). All references to this English translation are by paragraph number.

Chapter 1: The Human Experience of Worship

1. Joseph Martos, *Doors to the Sacred: A Historical Introduction to Sacraments in the Catholic Church* (Tarrytown, New York: Triumph Books, 1991), 3.
2. Ibid., 3–17.
3. Ibid.

Chapter 2: The Religious Experience of Worship

1. Cf. *CCC,* #1115.
2. Nathan D. Mitchell, *Eucharist as Sacrament of Initiation* (Chicago, Illinois: Liturgy Training Publications, 1994), 5–45.
3. James W. Fowler, *Weaving the New Creation: Stages of Faith and the Public Church* (Harper San Francisco: 1991), 85–86.
4. Francis Schussler Fiorenza, "Thy Kingdom Come," *Church* (Summer 1994): 5–9.

5. Thomas Merton, *Thoughts in Solitude* (New York: The Noonday Press, 1958), 17–21.

6. A. G. Martimort, ed., *The Church at Prayer* (Collegeville, Minnesota: The Liturgical Press, 1986), vol. 2, *The Eucharist,* by Robert Cabbie, 18–19.

7. Cf. *CCC,* #2097.

8. Patrick Bishop, S.J., "Worship," in *The New Dictionary of Sacramental Worship,* ed. Peter E. Fink, S.J. (Collegeville, Minnesota: The Liturgical Press, 1990), 1331–32.

9. Richard P. McBrien, *Catholicism* (New York: Harper-Collins Publishers, 1994), 787–96.

10. Cf. *CCC,* #1116.

11. Andrew M. Greeley, *The Catholic Myth: The Behavior and Beliefs of American Catholics* (New York: Charles Scribner's Sons, 1990), 34–64.

12. Cf. *CCC,* #1123 and 1124.

13. See, for example, Eugene J. Fisher, ed., *The Jewish Roots of Christian Liturgy* (New York/Mahwah, N.J.: Paulist Press, 1990) and the *Catechism of the Catholic Church,* #1096.

Chapter 3: The Rite of Christian Initiation of Adults

1. National Council of Catholic Bishops, *Rite of Christian Initiation of Adults* (Chicago: Liturgy Training Publications, 1988), #2.

2. Cf. *CCC,* #1212.

3. Thomas J. Rausch, S.J., "Discipleship," in *The New Dictionary of Catholic Spirituality,* ed. Michael Downey (Collegeville, Minnesota: The Liturgical Press, 1993), 281–84.

4. McBrien, *Catholicism,* 810–11.

5. Martos, *Doors to the Sacred,* 176.

6. *Rite of Christian Initiation of Adults,* #14.

7. Cf. *CCC,* #1234–45.

Chapter 4: Baptism

1. Cf. *CCC,* #1252.

2. William J. Bausch, *A New Look at the Sacraments* (Mystic, Connecticut: Twenty-Third Publications, 1983), 65–66.
3. NCCB, *Rite for the Baptism of Children* (New York: Catholic Book Publishing Company, 1969), #3.
4. Ibid., #56.
5. Ibid., #65.
6. Ibid., #68.
7. Bausch, 82–84.

Chapter 5: Confirmation

1. Cf. *CCC,* #1286–88.
2. Bausch, 93.
3. Cf. *CCC,* #1290–92.
4. NCCB, *The Rites of the Catholic Church,* vol. 1 (New York: The Liturgical Press, 1976), 472–78.
5. *The Rites of the Catholic Church,* #12 and 5.
6. Ibid., #22.
7. Ibid., #25.
8. Ibid., #27.

Chapter 6: Eucharist

1. Cf. *CCC,* #1337–38.
2. Cf. *CCC,* #1340.
3. Cf. *CCC,* #1362–64.
4. Cabbie, *The Eucharist,* 13.
5. Ibid., 14.
6. Ibid., 14–16
7. Richard P. McBrien, ed., *The HarperCollins Encyclopedia of Catholicism* (Harper San Francisco: 1995), 484–85.
8. Cf. *CCC,* #1378–79.
9. McBrien, 485.
10. Dennis C. Smolarski, S.J., *Sacred Mysteries: Sacramental Principles and Liturgical Practice* (New York/Mahwah, N.J.: Paulist Press, 1995), 71.
11. NCCB, *The Sacramentary* (New York: Catholic Book Publishing Company, 1985), 19–50.

12. GIRM, #58.
13. GIRM, #60.
14. GIRM, #9, 34.
15. GIRM, #101.
16. Cf. *CCC*, #1352–54.
17. "The Constitution on the Sacred Liturgy," in *Vatican Council II: The Conciliar and Post Conciliar Documents*, ed. Austin Flannery, O.P. (Northport, New York: Costello Publishing Company, 1987), #2.
18. Megan McKenna, "Stories and Memories of Christmas," *Church* 8 (Winter 1992): 5–6.
19. Catherine Vincie, R.S.H.M., "The Liturgical Assembly: Review and Reassessment," *Worship* 67 (March 1993): 144.
20. Fowler, *Weaving the New Creation: Stages of Faith and the Public Church*, 147–89.
21. For a discussion of this issue see Bishop Michael Sheehan, "Sunday Worship Without a Priest," *Origins* (March 5, 1992): 621–25.
22. Vatican II, *Constitution on the Sacred Liturgy*, #14.

Chapter 7: Reconciliation

1. Cf. Mk 1:15, Mt 3:2, Lk 4:18.
2. Cf. *CCC*, #1485 and Lk 20:19–23.
3. Cf. Mk 2:7, Mk 2:5, 10, Lk 7:48.
4. Cf. *CCC*, #1461.
5. Cf. *CCC*, #1440.
6. Cf. Acts 2:38–39.
7. Cf. *CCC*, #1434–39.
8. NCCB, *The Rite of Penance* (New York: Catholic Book Publishing Company, 1975), #2.
9. Cf. *CCC*, #1436.
10. Bausch, 155–57.
11. NCCB, *The Sacramentary*, 358–59.
12. Ibid., 360–64.
13. Peter E. Fink, S.J., "Liturgies of Reconciliation," in *The New Dictionary of Sacramental Worship*, ed. Peter E. Fink,

S.J. (Collegeville, Minnesota: The Liturgical Press, 1990), 1044.
14. McBrien, *Catholicism*, 837–38.
15. Ibid., 839–40.
16. Bausch, 188–92.
17. NCCB, *The Rite of Penance*, 8.
18. Ibid., 14–15.
19. Ibid., 40.
20. Ibid., 33–41.
21. Ibid., 44–71.
22. Cf. *CCC*, #1483.
23. NCCB, *The Rite of Penance*, 74–78.
24. James Dallen, "Sacrament of Reconciliation," in *The New Dictionary of Sacramental Worship*, ed. Peter E. Fink, S.J. (Collegeville, Minnesota: The Liturgical Press, 1990), 1061.
25. Beverly A. Nitschke, "Confession and Forgiveness: The Continuing Agenda," *Worship* 68 (July 1994): 368.

Chapter 8: Anointing of the Sick and Viaticum

1. Cf. Mk 1–3.
2. Cf. *CCC*, #1500–01.
3. Cf. *CCC*, #1525.
4. Mk 16:18.
5. Mt 25:31–46.
6. McBrien, *Catholicism*, 843–44.
7. Bausch, 206–7.
8. Charles W. Gusmer, "Anointing of the Sick," in *The New Dictionary of Theology*, eds. Joseph A. Komonchak, Mary Collins, Dermot A. Lane (Wilmington, Delaware: Michael Glazier, Inc., 1987), 24.
9. McBrien, 845.
10. Bausch, 209–10.
11. McBrien, 847.
12. Cf. NCCB, *The Rites of the Catholic Church*, vol. 1, pp. 758–908.
13. Ibid., 778–79.

14. Ibid., 780.
15. Ibid., 790.
16. Ibid., 825.
17. Ibid., 831–39.
18. Ibid., 844–45.
19. Ibid., 855.
20. Ibid., 857.
21. Cf. *CCC*, #1520–23.
22. 2 Cor 12:9.

Chapter 9: Marriage

1. Martos, *Doors to the Sacred*, 344.
2. Ibid., 343–44.
3. Genesis 1:1–3:24.
4. *Code of Canon Law: Latin-English Edition* (Washington, D.C.: Canon Law Society of America, 1983), #1055.
5. Cf. *CCC*, #1602.
6. Cf. Mk 10:1–12; Mt 16:18.
7. Martos, *Doors to the Sacred*, 348.
8. Cf. *CCC*, #1612; Jn 2:1–11.
9. Cf. *CCC*, #1616 and Eph 5:25–26, 31–32.
10. Bausch, *A New Look at the Sacraments*, 214–15.
11. Proverbs 5:15–20.
12. McBrien, *Catholicism*, 854–55.
13. Ibid., 855–56.
14. Vatican II, *Pastoral Constitution on the Church in the Modern World*, #50.
15. McBrien, *Catholicism*, 856–58.
16. Cf. *CCC*, #1660–66.
17. NCCB, *The Rites of the Catholic Church*, vol. 1, 715–58.
18. Ibid., 949–57.
19. Ibid., #47.
20. Ibid., #48.
21. Ibid., #49.
22. Ibid., #52.
23. Ibid., #12–18.
24. Ibid., #23.

25. Ibid., #25.
26. Ibid., #26.
27. Ibid., #47.
28. James A. Coriden, "Annulment," in *The Modern Catholic Encyclopedia* (Collegeville, Minnesota: The Liturgical Press, 1994), 31–32.

Chapter 10: Orders

1. Martos, *Doors to the Sacred,* 393–94.
2. Cf. *CCC,* #1536–38.
3. Vatican II, *Dogmatic Constitution on the Church,* #18.
4. Ibid., #19.
5. Cf. Heb 5:1; Ex 29:1–30; Lev 8.
6. Cf. Heb 5:10; 6:20; 7:26; 10:14.
7. Vatican II, *Dogmatic Constitution on the Church,* #10; cf. *CCC,* #1546–47.
8. Cf. Paul Bernier, S.S.S., *Ministry in the Church: A Historical and Pastoral Approach* (Mystic, Connecticut: Twenty-Third Publications, 1992); William J. Rademacher, *Lay Ministry: A Theological, Spiritual and Pastoral Handbook* (New York: Crossroad Publishing Company, 1991).
9. Richard P. McBrien, *Ministry: A Theological, Pastoral Handbook* (San Francisco: Harper & Row Publishers, 1987), 12–13.
10. Cf. 1 Cor 12:4–11.
11. McBrien, *Catholicism,* 868–69.
12. Ibid., 870.
13. James K. Voiss, "Celibacy" in *The HarperCollins Encyclopedia of Catholicism,* ed. Richard P. McBrien (Harper San Francisco: 1995), 289–91.
14. McBrien, *Catholicism,* 870.
15. Ibid., 871.
16. NCCB, *The Rites of the Catholic Church,* vol. 2 (Collegeville, Minnesota: The Liturgical Press, 1980), 22–26.
17. Ibid., #12.
18. Ibid., #13.
19. Ibid., #14.

20. Ibid., #22.
21. Ibid., #26.
22. Ibid., #13.
23. Ibid., #18.

Chapter 11: The Ritual Life of the Parish

1. Cf. *CCC*, #1668.
2. Ibid., #1669–74.
3. Vatican II, *The Constitution of the Sacred Liturgy*, #60–61.
4. NCCB, *Order of Christian Funerals* (Collegeville, Minnesota: The Liturgical Press, 1989).
5. Ibid., #50, 51, 204.
6. Ibid., #398.
7. Ibid., #56.
8. Ibid., #129.
9. Ibid., #206.
10. Vatican II, *The Constitution on the Sacred Liturgy*, #100.
11. Joyce Ann Zimmerman, C.P.P.S., *Morning and Evening: A Parish Celebration* (Chicago, Illinois: Liturgy Training Publications, 1996), 9.
12. Stanislaus Campbell, F.S.C., "Liturgy of the Hours" in *The New Dictionary of Sacramental Worship*, ed. Peter E. Fink, S.J. (Collegeville, Minnesota: The Liturgical Press, 1990), 562–76.
13. *Christian Prayer: The Liturgy of the Hours* (New York: Catholic Book Publishing Company, 1976). See also various publications from Liturgy Training Publications, including their annual *At Home With the Word* and *Morning and Evening* (1996) by Joyce Ann Zimmerman and Kathleen Harmon.
14. Everett A. Diederich, S.J., "Eucharistic Worship Outside Mass," in *The New Dictionary of Sacramental Worship*, ed. Peter E. Fink, S.J. (Collegeville, Minnesota: The Liturgical Press, 1990), 459–62.
15. *Order for the Solemn Exposition of the Holy Eucharist* (Collegeville, Minnesota: The Liturgical Press, 1993), #2.
16. Ibid., #3 and 6.

17. Ibid., #50.
18. NCCB, *The Book of Blessings* (Collegeville, Minnesota: The Liturgical Press, 1989).
19. Ibid., #1 and 3.
20. Ibid., #6 and 7.
21. Ibid., #21.
22. Ibid., #26.
23. Ibid., #18.
24. Cf. *CCC,* #2651.
25. Michael S. Driscoll, "Cult of the Saints," in *The New Dictionary of Sacramental Worship,* ed. Peter E. Fink, S.J. (Collegeville, Minnesota: The Liturgical Press, 1990), 1143.
26. 1 Thessalonians 5:16–22.

Conclusion

1. Paul Bernier, S.S.S., *The Eucharist: Celebrating Its Rhythms in Our Lives* (Notre Dame, Indiana: Ave Maria Press, 1993), 51.
2. Lk 1:26–6:28.
3. Peter Conroy, "The Catechumenate and Today's Church," *Catechumenate* 18 (July 1996), 22.

Selected Bibliography

Bausch, William J. *A New Look at the Sacraments*. Mystic, Connecticut: Twenty-Third Publications, 1983.

Bernier, Paul. *Ministry in the Church: A Historical and Pastoral Approach*. Mystic, Connecticut: Twenty-Third Publications, 1992.

——. *The Eucharist: Celebrating Its Rhythms in Our Lives*. Notre Dame, Indiana: Ave Maria Press, 1993.

Catechism of the Catholic Church. Washington, D.C.: United States Catholic Conference, Inc., Libreria Editrice Vaticana, 1994.

Code of Canon Law: Latin-English Edition. Washington, D.C.: Canon Law Society of America, 1983.

Downey, Michael, ed. *The New Dictionary of Catholic Spirituality*. Collegeville, Minnesota: The Liturgical Press, 1993.

Fink, Peter E., ed. *The New Dictionary of Sacramental Worship*. Collegeville, Minnesota: The Liturgical Press, 1990.

Fisher, Eugene J., ed. *The Jewish Roots of Christian Liturgy*. New York/Mahwah, N.J.: Paulist Press, 1990.

Flannery, Austin, ed. *Vatican Council II: The Conciliar and Post Conciliar Documents*. Northport, New York: Costello Publishing Company, 1987.

Fowler, James W. *Weaving the New Creation: Stages of Faith and the Public Church*. Harper San Francisco, 1991.

Glazier, Michael, and Monika K. Hellwig, eds. *The Modern Catholic Encyclopedia.* Collegeville, Minnesota: The Liturgical Press, 1994.

Greeley, Andrew M. *The Catholic Myth: The Behavior and Beliefs of American Catholics.* New York: Charles Scribner's Sons, 1990.

Komonchak, Joseph A., Mary Collins, and Dermot A. Lane, eds. *The New Dictionary of Theology.* Wilmington, Delaware: Michael Glazier, Inc., 1987.

Lee, Bernard J., ed. *Alternative Futures for Worship.* 7 vols. Collegeville, Minnesota: The Liturgical Press, 1987.

Martimort, A. G., ed. *The Church at Prayer.* 4 vols. Collegeville, Minnesota: The Liturgical Press, 1986.

Martos, Joseph. *Doors to the Sacred: A Historical Introduction to Sacraments in the Catholic Church.* Tarrytown, New York: Triumph Books, 1991.

McBrien, Richard P. *Catholicism.* New York: HarperCollins Publishers, 1994.

———. *The HarperCollins Encyclopedia of Catholicism.* Harper San Francisco, 1995.

———. *Ministry: A Theological, Pastoral Handbook.* San Francisco: Harper and Row Publishers, 1987.

Merton, Thomas. *Thoughts in Solitude.* New York: The Noonday Press, 1958.

Mitchell, Nathan D. *Eucharist as Sacrament of Initiation.* Chicago, Illinois: Liturgy Training Publications, 1994.

National Conference of Catholic Bishops. *The Rites of the Catholic Church.* 3 vols. New York: The Liturgical Press, 1976.

———. *The Sacramentary.* New York: Catholic Book Publishing Company, 1985.

———. *Order of Christian Funerals*. Collegeville, Minnesota: The Liturgical Press, 1989.

———. *Christian Prayer: The Liturgy of the Hours*. New York: Catholic Book Publishing Company, 1976.

———. *Order for the Solemn Exposition of the Holy Eucharist*. Collegeville, Minnesota: The Liturgical Press, 1993.

———. *The Book of Blessings*. Collegeville, Minnesota: The Liturgical Press, 1989.

———. *Rite of Christian Initiation of Adults*. Chicago, Illinois: Liturgy Training Publications, 1988.

Rademacher, William J. *Lay Ministry: A Theological, Spiritual and Pastoral Handbook*. New York: Crossroad Publishing Company, 1991.

Smolarski, Dennis C. *Sacred Mysteries: Sacramental Principles and Liturgical Practice*. New York/Mahwah, N.J.: Paulist Press, 1995.

Talley, Thomas J. *The Origins of the Liturgical Year*. Collegeville, Minnesota: The Liturgical Press, 1986.

Zimmerman, Joyce Ann. *Morning and Evening: A Parish Celebration*. Chicago, Illinois: Liturgy Training Publications, 1996.